The Black Muslim movement has produced a Negro who is alienated, militant, unforgiving. A Negro who wants to segregate, who desires no part of the white world, who is strengthened in this position by his consuming racial pride and his sense of destiny.

Why do the black Muslims take no part in the Negro Revolt? What is their relationship to Islam? Who is Elijah Muhammad and how did he come to power? What does Malcolm X hope to accomplish with his incendiary hate-the-white speeches?

Writing from a thorough knowledge of Black Muslim groups, Louis E. Lomax examines the entire movement—from its beginnings under its mysterious founder, W. D. Fard, to its present position as an explosive power on the racial scene. An important part of the book is devoted to the speeches of Malcolm X and Elijah Muhammad.

Recruited from the ranks of the criminal and destitute, the Black Muslims have become a sternly moral and self-respecting people. Their indictment of White America cannot be denied. They are a chilling example of what can happen when the Negro learns to hate.

A REPORT ON ELIJAH MUHAMMAD, MALCOLM X,
AND THE BLACK MUSLIM WORLD

when the
word
is given...

LOUIS E. LOMAX

GREENWOOD PRESS, PUBLISHERS
WESTPORT, CONNECTICUT

Library of Congress Cataloging in Publication Data

Lomax, Louis E   1922–
   When the word is given.

   Reprint of the ed. published by New American Library,
New York.
   Bibliography: p.
   1. Black Muslims. I. Title.
[BP272.L6 1979   297'.87   78-14002
ISBN 0-313-21002-0

Reprinted with the permission of the New American Library, Inc.

Reprinted in 1979 by Greenwood Press, Inc.
51 Riverside Avenue, Westport, CT 06880

Printed in the United States of America

10 9 8 7 6 5 4 3 2 1

To James Leonidas Lomax,
consecrated preacher, dedicated
teacher, and devoted parent.
What little love there is
among men today is due to
men like Uncle James.

CONTENTS

INTRODUCTION

THIS BOOK COMES at a time when the American race issue seems at a climax. Disturbing though it may be, it is encouraging that such a book as this can be written, that a group like the Black Muslims not only lives among us but that it can be investigated and studied. This means that at long last we are about to become honest about the race question. Negroes are saying what they think; white people are pausing to listen. These are the prerequisites of dialogue in a free society, and I predict that on the whole the Black Muslims will have a healthy influence on our social structure.

I know white people are frightened by Malcolm X and Elijah Muhammad; maybe now they will understand how I felt all my life, for there has never been a day when I was unafraid; we Negroes live our lives on the edge of fear, not knowing when or how the serpent of discrimination will strike and deprive us of something dear—a job here, a house there, an evening out over there, or a life itself. But things are better now than they once were; I am convinced they will soon be better than they are

now. I am optimistic because I feel Negroes are now determined to better their lot; I believe we will win because there is every evidence that white people are beginning to yield some of their power, and that— power—is what the argument is really about.

I have drawn on a spate of newspaper articles for this manuscript. I must give particular thanks to my friends Alex Haley and C. Eric Lincoln, Professor of Social Relations, Clark College, Atlanta. Haley's article on the Muslims and his unpublished notes were of immense help; Lincoln's book, *The Black Muslims in America,* is the definitive work on the followers of Elijah Muhammed and it was my bible as I tried first to understand and then to portray the Black Muslims. Dr. Lincoln and I shared research when he was preparing his fine work, and he has most graciously given me his consent to draw freely from his material, particularly that related to the origins and early history of the movement.

Thanks to Ann Westbay and Frances Hannah for their work as typists. Both of them also served as valuable critics as the manuscript took shape; for this additional service I owe them much appreciation.

Most of all I am indebted to the Black Muslims themselves. For more than four years, now, they have tolerated my questions and presence, knowing that I differ with them on many issues. Without their permission, over the years, this kind of book would have been impossible.

The summer of 1963 saw the Negro Revolt move into full view; it also saw the Black Muslims reach an almost incredible peak of public concern and notice. The intent of this work is to provide information and insight as companions to that concern. For correct information is the ultimate weapon of freedom. Even so, there are unpleasant and chilling things in this book. The Black Muslims—for some—are an unpleasant and chilling people, but freedom includes the right to be chilling, and the Black Muslims have no monopoly on unpleasantness.

In reality, Western man is on trial in this book. Without the failings of Western society, the Black Muslims

could not have come into being; without the continued failings of our society, the Black Muslims cannot endure. Here, then, Western white man, is a bitter pill. Do with it as you see fit.

LOUIS E. LOMAX

St. Albans, New York
July, 1963

THE COMING OF THE PROPHET

1. MAKE IT PLAIN,
MR. MINISTER!

The ultimate comment upon racialism in this republic is that the all-black Nation of Islam—a Chicago-based theocracy whose citizens are known as the Black Muslims—is one of the few religions ever produced by the American experience. Incensed liberals, Negro and white, will deny my assertion that the Black Muslims are a religious body, but the issue, both legally and theologically, has been settled: Courts in several states have ruled that the followers of The Honorable Elijah Muhammad are, indeed, adherents to a religious faith—as such, Black Muslim prison inmates have the right to hold services of worship as do other convicts. And no one who understands theologian Paul Tillich's argument that religion is nothing more than one's ultimate concern can doubt that the teachings of number-two Black Muslim leader, Malcolm X, constitute a religion.

Malcolm X is the St. Paul of the Black Muslim movement. Not only was he knocked to the ground by the bright light of truth while on an evil journey, but he also rose from the dust stunned, with a new name and a burning zeal to travel in the opposite direction and carry America's twenty million Negroes with him.

"This is the day of warning," Malcolm shouts to the Negro, "the hour during which prophecy is being fulfilled before your very eyes. The white man is doomed! Don't integrate *with* him, separate *from* him! Come ye out from among the white devils and be ye separate."

Nobody knows just how many Negroes have said "yes" to Malcolm X's call. Estimates of the Black Muslim membership vary from a quarter of a million down to fifty thousand. Available evidence indicates that about one hun-

15

dred thousand Negroes have joined the movement at one time or another, but few objective observers believe that the Black Muslims can muster more than twenty or twenty-five thousand active temple people.

The Black Muslims are feverish proselytizers, however, and they get amazing results from Negro prison inmates and the abandoned black masses who live in a world of despair and futility. Early commentators on the movement pointed to their work among prison inmates as further evidence that the Black Muslims were a dissolute lot. The opposite has proved to be true—the Muslims have been able to change the lives of these men once they emerge from prison. While the percentage of repeaters among ordinary Negro criminals runs very high, the Black Muslim converts seldom, if ever, return to a life of crime.

"Many of my followers—and ministers—were once criminals," Elijah Muhammad boasted in Washington, D.C., "but I changed all that by giving them knowledge of *self*. Once they discovered who the devil was and who God was, their lives were changed."

"All praise due to Allah," the crowd of some five thousand shouted as they leaped to their feet and applauded with rejoicing.

Non-Muslim Negroes used to scoff when Elijah wrote and talked about "knowledge of self." They are less apt to scoff now that a new wave of race pride has engulfed the Negro and a coterie of clean-cut, well-dressed, polite, and chillingly moral Black Muslim ex-convicts parade through the Negro community each day.

The same general approach, teaching race pride as knowledge of "self," accounts for the success the Black Muslims have among low-income Negroes. For these people are in something of a prison, too; they see themselves as failures and need some accounting for why they are what they are, why they are not what they are not. These needs are met when the wayward and the downtrodden sit at the feet of Malcolm X and hear him proclaim the divinity of the black man, hear him blame the white man for sin and lawlessness and then go on to herald the impending destruction of the "blue-eyed white devil."

Bean Pie and Beatitudes

The life of the Black Muslim centers around his temple
—sometimes called a mosque—and the temple restaurant.
They are usually located close together, in the heart of the
Negro ghetto, and are the nerve centers of work and worship. Temple services are held two or three times a week
and are generally preceded by family and group meals at
the restaurant. Families—most of them former Methodists
and Baptists—come in groups, the men dressed in black,
the women in flowing white, and the children wearing pins
or buttons to let the world know of their commitment to
The Honorable Elijah Muhammad.

The restaurants—like the Black Muslim homes—strictly
adhere to Moslem dietary laws. Muslim sisters glory in their
ability to prepare dishes that satisfy the traditional eating
habits of the American Negro without violating these laws.
The best example of imaginative Black Muslim cooking is
their famous bean pie, something of a gourmet's delight in
the Negro community. Negroes in New York have been
known to come to Harlem from miles around just to buy
a bean pie for the family table. The restaurants also serve
as business headquarters for the movement; they are the
distribution centers for Black Muslim newspapers and other
periodicals, the place where one is invited to have a talk
with a Black Muslim leader. Temple Number Seven Restaurant at 116th Street and Lenox Avenue in Harlem is
where Minister Malcolm X holds forth: he can be seen there
almost any time conducting the financial affairs of the
movement and holding press conferences. Then, on a sign
from one of his assistants, Malcolm bounds out of the
restaurant to conduct temple service at Temple Number
Seven, half a block away.

Throughout the nation the Muslims generally meet in
rented halls—a Masonic Temple in one town, over a pool
room in another. Men and women enter the temple together, but once in the vestibule the families are separated.
Everybody is searched thoroughly and all sharp objects, to

say nothing of weapons, are taken away. The search is carried out by well-trained sisters and brothers who work with
the efficiency of jail guards. They assign a small paper bag
to each worshiper, and such objects as nail files, pocket-
knives, scissors—any sharp objects that might conceivably
be used as weapons—are put into the bag for safe keeping
until the parishioner leaves the temple. Even the ordeal of
being searched is made palatable by a pleasant brother or
sister who explains that the visitor must be relieved of all
weapons because once the truth about the white man is
explained, the visitor might run out and start his private
Armageddon before the "word" comes.

The men and women are ushered into the temple through
separate doors and are ordered to sit on opposite sides. The
auditorium is generally a drab room, one used by many
groups in the course of a week. In Birmingham, Alabama,
for example, the Black Muslims use the Masonic Hall auditorium. The Sunday I visited the services there one could
see posters, fans, and other materials left by groups who
had used the same hall earlier in the week. The chairs of
the auditorium are arranged in rows, a wide gulf between
the "brothers" side and that of the "sisters." Dark-suited
young men, members of The Fruit of Islam, patrol the floor
incessantly. They dart about, nudging children to silence,
awakening a slumbering brother or sister, and performing
whatever duties might come to hand, all the while keeping
up a rapid-fire "That's right," "You tell it like it is," in
response to what the minister is saying.

The visitor finds himself inside a strange new world at a
Black Muslim service. Many religions separate men and
women during their services, but few Negroes are members
of such faiths and so they are intrigued from the outset.
Their sense of being in on something exotic, thus meaningful, is increased when one of the lesser ministers takes the
platform and says a few words in Arabic. The Negro is told
that this was his language before the white man kidnaped
his father and truncated his culture.

"As-Salaam-Alaikum!" the minister says—Peace be unto
you.

"Wa-Alaikum-Salaam," the visitor is taught to reply—
"Peace also be unto you."

The Black Muslims have little or no liturgy. They do not

sing in the temple, for they have not yet developed hymns that enunciate their faith. The nearest thing I have heard to a Black Muslim hymn is a plaintive and moving song written by Minister Louis X of Boston, "The White Man's Heaven Is the Black Man's Hell." It is often sung in the temples, but only as a solo by some gifted member of the congregation.

Many of the Black Muslims are excellent musicians; indeed, they are sidemen for some of the best-known jazz groups in the nation. I have been in temple meetings where a group of brothers set the stage for the service by playing a protracted jazz riff. The music was as complex and as far out as anything you would hear at New York's Five Spot Café or any other den of progressive jazz. As these accomplished jazz men play out their frustrations, the audience sits in cold silence. Sometimes the musicians come on a beat or a shading that strikes some common chord, and the Muslims smile slightly and nod at one another. When the music is done—it goes on and on until it runs down, just as it does in the jazz clubs—the congregation applauds, and somewhere a male voice can be heard to say, "All praise due to Allah!"

Then the stage is set for the "teaching." In lieu of the cross, the focus of the Black Muslims' religious service is a huge blackboard divided into two sections. On one side is a drawing of the American flag with the Christian cross superimposed on it. Under this flag is written, "Slavery, Suffering and Death." On the other side of the blackboard is the half-crescent symbol of Islam, and under it is written, "Freedom, Justice and Equality." Under both flags, running the full length of the blackboard, is the somber warning: "Which one will survive the War of Armageddon?"

And it is against this backdrop that the minister gets up to "teach." Each temple has its own minister, who is extremely well trained in what he is to say and do. And he does it well.

The Black Muslims have but one message: The white man is by nature evil, a snake who is incapable of doing right, a devil who is soon to be destroyed. Therefore, the black man, who is by nature divine and good, must separate from the white man as soon as possible, lest he share the white man's hour of total destruction.

This sermon, or "teaching," is the high point of the service, what everybody has come to hear. An air of expectancy runs through the crowd as the moment to begin the teaching approaches. This is stock drama for the Black Muslims whether the meeting be a national affair where Elijah himself is to speak or a local meeting where the temple minister is to teach.

This air of expectancy is set stirring by the second-in-command, who keeps up a running promise that something good is about to happen. As warm-up man for Elijah's Washington, D.C., speech, Malcolm X electrified a crowd of some five thousand in Uline Arena with this:

"You are here to get some good news."

"Make it plain."

"But you must remember that what is good news for some is bound to be bad news for others."

"All praise due to Allah," the people shouted back.

"What is good news for the sheep," Malcolm continued, "is bad news for the wolf!"

"Make it plain, Mr. Minister. Make it plain."

The good news, as everybody knew, was that Elijah would be there soon with a message of freedom for the "sheep" (the black man) and a message of destruction for the "wolf" (the white man).

The setting for local meetings is much the same. In New York Minister Henry X gets the crowd ready for Malcolm by saying, "We are here to receive a blessing. The truth is going to be told here this afternoon."

"All praises due to Allah."

"The Messenger's Minister will be here shortly with word from the man who saw God."

"Make it plain."

"The Minister is going to tell you who and what you are!"

"Say the word."

"Then he is going to tell you who and what the devil is!"

"Make it plain."

"Then he is going to show you why you had better hurry up and get out from among the devil before you get destroyed with him."

This brings the crowd to their feet, cheering. The side door to the upstairs temple swings open and Malcolm X, a tall, rawboned, Ichabod-Crane-looking man, strolls in

flanked by an Honor Guard. As he walks to the platform his light-skinned, granite face is stern. He looks and acts like a military officer who may give a fatal order any minute. His clothes, always a size or so too large, literally drape from his body, making him look more gaunt than he actually is.

"Big Red," as Malcolm was called when he was peddling prostitutes and dope on the streets of Harlem, is a dashing and handsome man. Women of all races and creeds are drawn to him. He speaks with an authority that is all but hypnotic.

"When I say the white man is a devil," Minister Malcolm shouts, "I speak with the authority of history."

"That's right," the people shout back.

"The record of history shows that the white men, as a people, have never done good."

"Say on, brother, say on."

"He stole our fathers and mothers from their culture of silk and satins and brought them to this land in the belly of a ship—am I right or wrong?"

"You are right; God knows you are right."

"He brought us here in chains—right?"

"Right."

"He has kept us in chains ever since we have been here."

"Preach on, Brother Minister, preach on."

"Now this blue-eyed devil's time has about run out!"

The people leap to their feet rejoicing.

"Now the fiery hell he has heaped upon others is about to come down on the white man!"

"All praise due to Allah," the people shout.

"God—we call him Allah—is going to get this white, filthy, hog-loving beast off our backs," Malcolm promises.

"Say on—yes, yes, yes . . ."

"God is going to hitch him to the plow and make him do his own dirty work."

"Yes, yes. Say on!"

"God is going to take over the garment district and make those white dogs push their own trucks."

Men in the audience jump up and down and shout their approval: "All praises due to Allah. Praise His holy name!"

"Now, now," Malcolm says, "calm down, because I want you to hear me. Now I want to tell you who God is. I

want you to understand who Allah is so you will know who is going to get this white, dope-peddling beast off your back."

Malcolm smiles. A ripple of laughter runs through the audience—you see, they know who Allah is; they know who God is; they know just who is going to get the white man off their backs. But they have come to hear Malcolm "make it plain" again.

"The Honorable Elijah Muhammad teaches us that God —Allah—is not a spook; we don't worship any ghost for a God. We don't believe in any dead God."

"That's right."

"Our God is a live God."

"Yes."

"He is walking around here with you, among you, in you."

"Yes," the people shout back.

"God is black, like you; God is oppressed, like you; He looks like you; He acts like you; He walks like you; He talks like you . . ."

By this time, the people are back on their feet cheering. But Malcolm has gone as far toward describing God as he will go for a while.

"Now," he says, "you have to listen with understanding to know what I am talking about."

"We with you."

"We don't let white devils in our meetings."

"No, no, no!"

"But we have to worry about some of you because the white man has messed up your mind so bad that some of you will run back and tell everything. That's why we can't tell you everything; that's why you have to listen carefully and with understanding if you are going to find out just who God is. But if He walks like you, and looks like you, and talks like you, and suffers like you; and if He is with you, in you, and all around you . . . then . . . well, you figure it out!"

The people, particularly the men, lift their voices in a long shout, for they have again been told that the black man, taken collectively, is God—Allah—that Allah will soon, now, destroy the devil, the white man.

Malcolm X, as he does three or four times each week,

has "made it plain." He has told black men that they—as God—must deliver themselves from the evils and hurts of the white man. And that, of course, is what they came to temple to hear.

On another Sunday afternoon the message will take a different form. Malcolm this time elects to make his famous "deaf, dumb, and blind" speech. I, for one, believe Malcolm is at his best when he deals with this issue.

The speech begins as Malcolm X literally heaps abuse on his audience.

"You are deaf, dumb, and blind," he tells them. "You are lost in the wilderness of North America, and the black man's new day has been delayed because of you. Now I am here to get you ready."

"Make it plain," the people shout back.

"Now the first thing you must do is clean yourself up."

"Yes, that's right, that's right!"

"You must clean yourself up both physically and morally."

"That's right! That's right!"

"You must learn that certain foods are unclean. The hog is a filthy beast, and it is against God's will for you to eat it."

"That's right."

"You can never clean yourself up as long as you have hog in your body."

"Make it plain; make it plain."

"Then you must clean yourself up morally."

"That's right, Brother Minister, that's right."

"This white devil is responsible for all the dope and prostitution you see here among us."

"That's right."

"He has filled us with his immorality."

"All praise due to Allah."

"He has so confused us that our community is filled with addicts, thieves, and prostitutes."

"That's right."

"And you will notice," Malcolm continues, "that these are Christians who are dealing in dope and prostitution.

"And you and I know this is true because when we were Christians we used dope."

"Yes."

"We lied."

"Yes."

"We stole."

"Yes."

"We were unfaithful to our wives."

"Yes."

"We did everything antisocial and immoral."

"That's right."

"But now that we know who God is, now that we have found Allah—our original true God—now that we have learned love and respect for self, now that all this has happened, we have cleaned ourselves up."

"All praises due to Allah."

"We love our own black women."

"Yes."

"We protect our women and children from the devil and his works."

"Yes."

"And we have stopped turning the other cheek!"

"Yes."

"We respect authority, but we are ready to fight and die in defense of our lives."

"All praises due to Allah!"

Broadsides at Christianity delivered by Malcolm X and other ministers seem to make the strongest impression on the audience. The minister explains that the Negro was introduced to Christianity while a slave, a bondsman to the man who taught him about Jesus. Employing any history text, he reads at length, using "the white man's own writings to show that Christianity is a white man's religion." This strikes home, because the average Negro has read enough to know that there is a good deal of historical soundness in what the minister says. Then the minister goes on to point out that the Christian church (and they quote Adam Clayton Powell on this) "is the most segregated institution in America." And the Negro does not need a history book to know that this statement has total validity.

Then the minister goes on to attack Christianity on the grounds that its practitioners are immoral. He calls the roll of criminals and public failures, making much of the fact that they are "all Christians." The minister uses clippings from the newspapers showing white clergymen and church-goers either sanctioning segregation or being neutral about

it. During the Birmingham crisis I attended the Black Muslim service and saw Minister James X deliver a devastating indictment of Christianity simply by showing pictures of Birmingham Negroes being turned away from white churches. One picture showed the rebuffed Negroes praying on the church steps while white bullies, their fists balled up, stood near-by.

Black Christians are also indicted for immorality; the minister points out that "All of us were once in the church and we did everything evil." I have watched this argument at work and come away amazed at the way the Black Muslims take the Christian ethic as a measuring stick; they then arouse the guilt complex of the wayward Christians in the audience and then go on to blame Christianity for the individual's moral failure. This, to be sure, is a contorted argument. But it works. Christians sit in the temple audience and confess their Christian failing, then they repent themselves right out of the Christian church.

After the sermon the visitors are asked to raise any questions that may trouble them. The ministers deal with each question in detail, but the Black Muslim ushers (The Fruit of Islam) make certain the questioner is not an "agitator," someone who has come into the temple just to start a philosophical or theological argument.

"You are in here to be taught, Brother," I heard one Black Muslim say to a visitor, "not to argue." And when the visitor frankly says he does not understand what the Black Muslims are up to, or that, after honestly trying, he is unable to agree, the minister explains that this is not to be held against the visitor. "You are among the deaf, dumb, and blind," the minister explains kindly. Then he assures the visitor that further study and estrangement from "the teaching of the devil" will open his eyes and ears.

The climax of each temple service comes when visitors are invited to join the movement. There is great rejoicing when converts come forth. Eric Lincoln, who has attended more of these services than I have, says that the larger temples average a dozen or so converts at each meeting.

Once the visitor decides to join the temple, he is given a letter he must copy by hand:

                                    Address
                                    City and State
                                    Date

Mr. W. F. Muhammad
4807 South Woodlawn Avenue
Chicago 15, Illinois
Dear Savior Allah, Our Deliverer:
    I have been attending the teachings of Islam by one of
your Ministers, two or three times. I believe in it, and I
bear witness that there is no God but Thee, and that
Muhammad is Thy Servant and Apostle. I desire to re-
claim my Own. Please give me my Original name. My
slave name is as follows:

                                    Name
                                    Address
                                    City and State

    This letter of application is dispatched to Chicago, and
if the copy contains no errors, the visitor is sent a detailed
questionnaire that inquires into his family and employment
status. This completed, the applicant is given a thorough
investigation by local members of The Fruit. If the applicant stands muster, he is admitted to membership in the
Black Muslim movement.
    Then, and only then, is the convert allowed to drop his
"slave" name. If his name is, say, John King, he becomes
John X; if there are other Johns in the local temple, his
"X" will denote that he is the third, fourth, or whatever
number John to join that particular temple. Thus it is very
common to find John 2X or John 7X. Lincoln discovered a
midwestern Muslim whose name was John 17X. The "X"
is the Black Muslim's way of saying that his own origins—
before the white man—and name are a mystery; it is also
the Muslim's shout that he is an "ex," and "no longer what
I was when the white man had me deaf, blind, and dumb."
    I have sat with Black Muslims during temple meetings
and have seen the people, particularly the young children,
come alive with a new sense of identity; they seem to have
a new reason to go out and do battle with the rats and
roaches in the slums that are their homes. A feeling of unity

and love for one another grips the entire room as they silently stand to be dismissed.

They stretch forth their hands, palms upward, and in the name of Allah, the most powerful and all-merciful God, they vow to go in peace. But every Black Muslim temple meeting is saturated with expectation. It reaches its peak when the minister makes the promise that the War of Armageddon is drawing closer and closer. No one ever really says it, but there is an intense feeling that one day soon, at just such a meeting, the "word"—probably from Elijah Muhammad but through Malcolm X—will be given. Just what the word is nobody says; just what will happen when the word is given nobody seems to know. Yet everybody—man, woman, and child—is determined to be on hand when the "word" comes.

Such meetings as these have been going on all over the nation for several years. Most of us heard talk about the "temple people," as the Black Muslims were called, but there was very little real information about them. Nobody seemed to know just how many temple people there were, how they were organized, what they were really about. The consensus was that they were just another offbeat sect, one of the scores of "Islamic" movements that have sought to convert American Negroes during the past century. We had no idea of the power of the Black Muslims as a religious and political organization capable of rallying mass support. But early in 1959 we got the message.

The Alert Is Given

Shortly after dark on the night of April 14, 1958, police at Harlem's 28th Precinct received what had all the appearances of a routine call—a fight between two Negroes at the corner of 125th Street and Seventh Avenue. The dispatch officer barked into his microphone, and his orders squawked out in a dozen radio cars patrolling the area. The cars, their revolving red lights glaring, sped to the scene of the incident. Police poured out of the cars, their

clubs at the ready, and began to batter their way through the mob that had gathered.

One Johnson Hinton, a man nobody knew and who had nothing to do with the fight, was one of the spectators who had stopped to watch the melee. The police shoved and knocked aside several Negroes and finally came upon Hinton. What happened then is still a matter of argument, but one fact is agreed upon by all concerned: Hinton and the police entered into a verbal exchange and a policeman knocked Hinton to the ground, his head split open. A police ambulance was called and police took the position that another Negro agitator had been subdued. But they were in for a major surprise, and the city was on the brink of a race riot. Hinton, it turned out, was a Black Muslim, Johnson X, a member of Malcolm's Temple Number Seven in Harlem.

Within minutes after Hinton hit the ground the word spread that a Black Muslim had been assaulted by the police. An hour later some five hundred sullen, angry Black Muslim men put a cordon around the 28th Precinct Station House where Hinton was being held. This meant trouble, and plenty of it. Precinct Captain McGowan realized he had the makings of a riot on his hands and sent out an urgent call for responsible Negroes to rush to the scene and intervene. One of the first to arrive was James Hicks, editor of *The Amsterdam News,* a Harlem newspaper. Hicks accurately sized up the situation and told Captain McGowan that only one man, Minister Malcolm X, could manage the crowd and get them to disperse.

The police captain asked, in essence, "Who he?"

Shortly afterward Captain McGowan found out just who Malcolm X was. Flanked by several strapping, angry Muslim brothers, Malcolm walked into the station house. As he entered the door, he gave a sign, and the hundreds of Muslim brothers surrounding the area knew their stand was affirmed. The call went out for still more Muslim brothers to converge upon the area.

Once inside the station, Malcolm X sat down for hard bargaining. First, there was the matter of Brother Johnson Hinton lying on the floor of a jail cell with his head split open. Malcolm demanded that Hinton be given immediate hospital treatment. This was agreed to. Then Malcolm went on to place on record the facts of the affair. Johnson was

standing on the street, he was not involved in the fight, he at no time disobeyed a police order, and the police struck him out of sheer flailing frustration.

As Johnson Hinton was carried out of the station to an ambulance, Malcolm walked out the door and paused at the top of the steps. The dimly lit night was filled with Black Muslims and onlookers. Malcolm made a slight gesture, and, according to both police and editor Hicks, in exactly three minutes the streets were empty. The hundreds of Muslims simply vanished—at least the police thought they had vanished. In actuality they shifted their cordon to the hospital where Hinton was being treated. And it was only after Malcolm emerged from the hospital and gave another sign that the Black Muslims finally dispersed to their various homes.

"No man," Police Captain McGowan said to James Hicks, "should have that much power over that many people. We cannot control this town if one man can wield that kind of power."

Johnson Hinton now walks around with a silver plate in his head. An all-white jury awarded him seventy-five thousand dollars in damages against the City of New York. Those knowledgeable about the case and the Black Muslims feel that seventy-five thousand dollars is a small fee to pay for the service Malcolm X rendered the city that night. As the jury found, the police were absolutely wrong, and as Negroes know, Hinton's was only one of the Negro heads that are cracked open without reason by the New York police each year.

But there was a difference between Johnson Hinton and all the other Negroes who get their heads split open in Harlem: Hinton had black brothers and sisters who cared about him; he was a member of a tightly knit congregation of believers whose basic tenet is "fight in defense of your life" and whose main social ethic is "be ready to exact justice when one of your brothers is abused." The Muslims will deny it, but they have a "crisis system" that moves into action whenever a Muslim is abused. It involves a telephone pyramid—one man calls ten people and each of them calls ten—that in one hour can produce upward of a thousand Muslims at any given point in New York.

And the night Johnson Hinton's head was split open was the night New York police officials went into a huddle and named the Black Muslims, particularly Malcolm X, as people to watch.

Malcolm X brought unity to the black community in Harlem

2. FROM MOSES TO
MALCOLM X

The Black Muslims have been in the national spotlight for only four years now, although the movement itself was born more than a quarter of a century ago. It attracted some attention in Chicago and Detroit but did not emerge as a national concern until Minister Malcolm X, then serving as leader of the New York Muslims and as a sort of roving bishop for the entire movement, burst upon the scene.

As is all too often the case with white people, the Establishment took one look at the Black Muslims and lurched from apathy to frenzy. No one paused long enough to study just what the Muslims believe, what makes them a religion, how they function as a religion. One of the reasons why this has not been done is that the Establishment, both Negro and white, was afraid that open acceptance of the Black Muslims as a religion would legitimize them. Meanwhile, as I mentioned earlier, courts in several states have issued findings that the Muslims are, indeed, a religion, and as such enjoy the same freedom as, say, Roman Catholics.

But this is to get ahead of the story. In truth, the scheme of events, both economic and moral, that led to the formation of the Black Muslims first began to unravel on the west coast of Africa some five hundred years ago. And we must begin *there* and *then* if we are to understand clearly the *here* and *now*. Prior, and basic, to a full comprehension of the meaning of the Negro's African experience, we must pause and understand the role of religion in the life of a people.

31

The Negro as African and Tribesman

American Negro slaves were captured from the west
coast of Africa. They were by no means products of a
monolithic culture. They represented many tribes and sub-
tribes. They spoke a myriad of languages. Indeed, one of
the incredible ironies of the "Middle Passage" was that the
African slaves chained together in the hold of a boat as it
crossed the Atlantic were unable to talk to one another
because they did not have a common language. Yet these
were not uncivilized people. West Africans had developed
a complex society, as Lerone Bennett, Jr., suggests, long
before European penetration. Their political institutions,
rooted in family groupings, spiraled outward into village
states and empires. They had their armies and courts and,
if this is of any comfort to modern Americans, their own
internal-revenue departments. Speaking of Africa before
the European penetration, anthropologist Melville J.
Herskovits wrote, "Of the areas inhabited by non-literate
peoples Africa exhibits the greatest incidence of complex
governmental structure." Not even the kingdoms of Peru
and Mexico could mobilize resources and concentrate power
more effectively than could some of these African monarchies,
which are more to be compared with European states of the
Middle Ages than referred to in the common conception,
"primitive state."

Agriculture, herding, and artistry were important to the
West African, but the concept of private property was not
widely accepted. The land belonged to the community.
The core of West African society was the family. Interest-
ingly enough, most of the African tribes constructed their
families along matrilineal lines—the family tree was traced
through the mother. On the whole, the West Africans were
a mixture of various stocks by the time of the slave in-
vasions. Centuries of interbreeding had produced Africans
of varying shapes, colors, and features. Although they spoke
many languages, they approached a semblance of linguistic
unity in that only four of the African languages had been

reduced to writing before the coming of the white man.

Whatever their tongue or color the West Africans were a deeply religious people. No greater injustice has been done to a people than that committed by spurious American historical and anthropological writings which suggest that African religion should be written off as infantile animism. On the contrary, the West Africans had developed complex answers to such major tribal inquiries as "What is man?" "Who is God?" "What is life?" and "How final is death's sting?" At rock bottom, the religion of West Africa embraced a concept of "Life Forces." The "Life Force" of the Creator was present in all things animate and inanimate and was viewed as a particularized but microcosmic fragment of the Supreme Being, God, Who created the earth. As Lerone Bennett, Jr., suggests, this African concept of God as a vital force in everything bears a striking resemblance to Henri Bergson's "élan vital." Religion formed the center of West African life. Every event took on religious meaning. And there is no telling what towering civilization might have blossomed and survived there had the white man not made his intrusion.

Africans as Moslems

The character of this work demands that we examine the impact of Islam on the black Africans, particularly on those of the West Coast, if we are to understand and evaluate the current preachings of The Honorable Elijah Muhammad and Malcolm X.

Dr. John Hope Franklin feels that influences of the religion of Mohammed on the African way of life have been exaggerated. It seems certain that Mohammedanism had little influence upon black Africans prior to the fourteenth century. As early as the seventh century the Moslems swept from Arabia over into Egypt. Subsequently, they moved into North Africa with great success. But when they attempted to penetrate the land of the black African below the Sahara, they encountered complex resistance from the kingdoms of Ghana, Melle, and Songhay, where thriving

cultures were already in operation. Some Negro monarchs accepted Mohammedanism for economic or political reasons, but their subjects clung to their tribal religions. The Moslems were never able to win over the peoples of Melle, Hausa, Yoruba, and Susu despite the fact that Negroes were accepted as their equals. And when invited to enjoy both the economic and cultural advantages the religion offered, the masses of West African Negroes rejected Islam in favor of their own tribal way of life.

It is of singular significance that Christianity was already entrenched in North Africa when Mohammedanism made its appearance there in the seventh century. The two faiths became locked in a life-and-death struggle for the control of North Africa. But in West Africa, the region from which the bulk of the Negro slaves were taken, Christianity was all but unknown until the Portuguese and Spanish set up their missions in the sixteenth century. Almost from the onset Christianity was beset by moral ambivalence; on the one hand the Spanish and Portuguese missionaries espoused a doctrine of equality and brotherhood while on the other hand Spanish and Portuguese slave traders were seizing thousands of Africans and shipping them off to the New World to become slaves. It was thus aboard "The Good Ship Jesus" that the first slaves arrived in America. As John Hope Franklin comments, "If the natives of West Africa were slow to accept Christianity, it was not only because they were attached to their own particular form of tribal worship, but because it was beyond the capacity of the unsophisticated West African mind to reconcile the teaching of brotherhood and the practice of slavery by the white interlopers." The European Christians, however, found no conflict between Christ and slavery and by 1860 the twenty Negroes who landed at Jamestown in 1619 had become four million.

The Lord's Song in a Strange Land

The literature of the American Negro rumbles with the controversy over the transplantation, or lack of it, of African

culture. Some Africanisms have survived in the New World, particularly in the West Indies and in Haiti. But the impact of the New World culture upon the Africans—who were already culturally diffused—was decisive.

What happened to the African is exemplified by the pious captain who held prayer service twice a day on his slave ship. After the prayer services were over, he retired to his cabin and wrote the now-famous hymn which begins "How sweet the Name of Jesus sounds in a believer's ear, it quells the sorrow, drowns his fears, and drives away his tears." Further evidence of the complete Americanization of the African lies in the fact that descendants of the first Negro slaves—Negro Christians born in Spain and Portugal—settled in the New World long before the *Mayflower* came. These Negroes were explorers, not slaves. Some of them accompanied the French into the Mississippi Valley, and others went with the Portuguese into South America. Thirty Negroes were with Balboa when he discovered the Pacific Ocean, and several were with Menéndez as he marched into Florida.

The bulk of the Negroes in America are descendants, at least partially, of Africans who arrived in this country first as indentured servants and who were then lowered into slavery. It was under the aegis of slavery that the black American accepted Jehovah as his God. It is this ignominious first meeting between Jesus and the black American that Malcolm X probes so accurately and exploits so effectively.

Christ and His Cotton Curtain

When the Black Muslims call upon American Negroes to forsake Christianity and return to Islam, they not only flirt with historical inaccuracy, but they declare open war against the Negro church, which has been properly described by E. Franklin Frazier as the most important institution the American Negro has built. That the Black Muslims have had remarkable success in leading thousands of Negroes out of the Christian church and into the tem-

ples of Islam is clear evidence that somewhere in the history of American Christendom faith failed the Negro. And when it is realized that the Black Muslims are able to attract three times as many fellow travelers as they do members, the failure of Christianity becomes even more pronounced. How and why that failure came about lies deep in the swamps and plantations of the South, and we must return there and examine the record of that failure if we are to grasp fully the meaning of Malcolm X when he says, "Christianity is a white man's religion."

Every people has a sense of the past, the handed-down record of what has gone before, the Ark of the Covenant, as the collective experience of a people. For the American Negro this sense of the past begins in America, not Africa, for it was in America that the American Negro was forged into a people. Under the tutelage of white plantation masters the first slaves discovered a common language that made it possible for them to communicate with each other and thus make a collective expression of their resentment of the peculiar institution known as slavery. The white slave owner was Christian, and despite some efforts to prohibit Negro exposure to the Bible, most slave masters or, more particularly, their wives—saw to it that the slaves heard the gospel. One of the moving scenes of American history is that of slave and slave master gathered together in church on the plantation to hear the gospel of a Christ of brotherhood. Most plantation masters saw to it that the minister kept his sermon confined to such texts as "Servants, be obedient to them that are your masters" (Ephesians 6:5). There was a deeper meaning for the slave in the religious life of the plantation. Strangely enough, it was the Old Testament with its rich history of the Jews and their bouts with famines, pestilence, idolatry, and slavery that attracted the imagination of the religious slave. Working in the field by day, having his wife sold away from him down the river to another plantation, seeing his son stripped naked to the waist and given a hundred lashes for being "uppity," the Negro slave found a cruel parallel between his life and that of those who begged favor to let them return to their homeland and who finally were delivered by God, who visited a series of disasters upon the slave master. Here in the Negro plantation church—called by scholars "The In-

visible Institution"—the Negro began to translate the history of the Jews into words of deliverance and hope. It was
thus that slaves began to translate the social history of the
Jews into Negro spirituals:

Didn't my Lord deliver Daniel?

*Go down, Moses, way down in Egypt land, tell Old
Pharaoh let my people go . . .*

*We are climbing Jacob's ladder, every round goes higher
and higher. . . . Soldiers of the Cross*

*Jordan's river is chilly and cold, none can cross but the
true and bold . . .*

*Swing low, sweet chariot, coming for to carry me
home . . .*

*Soon I will be done with the troubles of the world, going
home to live with God . . .*

At first it appeared that the American church would embrace integration of the Negro and lead the attack against
the institution of slavery. In 1784, for example, the Methodist Church declared slavery "contrary to the golden laws
of God" and went on to order its members to set all slaves
free within twelve months. But Southern states led by Virginia forced a suspension of the resolution. Five years later
the Baptist Church passed pretty much the same resolution.
But it, too, recanted under pressure from the Deep South.
Even so, many churches accepted Negroes as parishioners,
though many whites feared that they could be flirting with
disaster if they adopted a truly liberal policy with respect
to Negro membership. By the same token, they were leery
of all Negro churches on the plantation. They feared that
Negro ministers and church officials would exercise considerable authority over their slave communicants and thus
the church could become a center of rebellion. The American church was having other problems at the time, and its
concern with the Negro question was not prime. The
Anglican clergy, flouting their Toryism, were causing many

American parishioners to seek complete disassociation from the Church of England. In fact, every religious denomination, with the exception of the Roman Catholic, was busy establishing an American wing of its church in the hope that it would be completely separate from its European sponsor. The Catholic Church itself finally acquiesced and became separate under the control of a special Prefect Apostolic. This intercontinental war between the churches of the New World and the Old eclipsed the problem of the Negro as far as white churchmen were concerned and set the scene for the establishment of separate churches for Negroes.

Negro Baptist churches began to sprout while the war for independence was still being waged. George Liele, a Negro leader, founded a Baptist church in Savannah, Georgia, in 1779 that became the nucleus of the Negro Baptists in that state. Virginia Negroes organized a Baptist church in Petersburg in 1776, in Richmond in 1780, and in Williamsburg in 1785. According to Dr. John Hope Franklin, many of the white clergy in Virginia assisted Negroes in setting up and organizing their separate churches.

It was in the North that the Negro church really burgeoned. Foremost among the Northern Negro churchmen was Richard Allen, an ex-slave who had purchased his freedom from his Delaware master in 1777, the year he also accepted Christ as his saviour. In 1786 Allen moved to Philadelphia and began to hold prayer meetings for Negroes. His efforts to establish a Negro church were opposed by whites and some Negroes. But when the officials of St. George's Church, where Allen frequently preached, began to segregate a large number of Negroes who came to hear him, it became clear to Allen's Negro detractors that the time was right for a Negro church. The final break came when white church officials pulled Allen, Absalom Jones, and William White from their knees while they were praying in what had been set aside as the white section of the church. An innately dramatic man, Allen led the Negroes out of St. George's Church and organized Mother Bethel, now the central church of Negro Methodism. Allen and his followers organized what became the African Methodist Episcopal Church and by 1820 they had four thousand followers in

Philadelphia alone. The organization spread as far west as Pittsburgh and as far south as Charleston.

In New York City, because of discrimination and segregation Negroes withdrew from the John Street Methodist Episcopal Church and established what is now the African Methodist Episcopal Zion Church, one of whose leading bishops is Dr. Stephen Gill Spottswood, the current chairman of the board of the NAACP. The same trend was developing among Negro Baptists of the North. In 1809 thirteen Negro members of a white Baptist church in Philadelphia were dismissed to form a church of their own. The Negro Baptists of Boston set up their own church in the same year under the leadership of Reverend Thomas Paul. At the same time he was shepherding the Boston congregation, Rev. Paul also organized a Negro Baptist church in New York City. The church was later named Abyssinian and is now pastored by the controversial minister-politician, Adam Clayton Powell, Jr.

Both white and Negro clergymen agree that the development of separate churches was inconsistent with the teachings of religion, but the Negro clergymen were adamant, feeling that a separate church would give them an opportunity to develop leadership. More, there were theological points that Negro churchmen found difficult to accept. One was the notion, widely held among white Christians particularly in the South, that the Negro was the descendant of Ham, the son of Noah, who laughed at his father's nakedness and thus doomed himself and his descendants to be hewers of wood and drawers of water—that is to say, servants—to the descendants of Noah's other sons. This theological justification for the concept of Negro inferiority reached its peak during the early part of the nineteenth century, when a spurious body of anthropological and biological scholarship offered "scientific proof" of the Negro's innate inferiority both as a spiritual being and as a person. It was the "Linnaean Web" that did it: scientists at that time completely embraced the notions of Linnaeus that the classification of peoples in terms of skull sizes and shapes as well as in terms of color was the first step toward knowledge. The American scene of the early 1800s was peopled with a variety of racial stocks, and the majority of the white Protestant group fell victims of the all-too-easy temptation

to judge the worth of an individual merely by looking at the color of his skin or the shape of his nose. Thus, the image of the hook-nosed Jewish peddler; the drunken, shiftless Irishman; the stupid, soggy German; the hot-tempered Italian; and the ragged, lazy Negro.

Only in the Negro church, then, did the Negro find a sense of dignity and meaning. Only there was he made to feel a true and equal child of God. The Negro church developed a peculiar theology that spoke to the frustration of the American Negro, and it was there that the Negro translated Christianity into the hope of Negro deliverance.

But two factors, hardly noticed at the time, were to keep the Negro church from becoming a completely closed institution: first, the Negro church was a part of the Negro community, which was an affront to every sensitive Negro citizen; the Negro community was an enclave of terror and police brutality, and the growing ambition of every Negro was somehow to escape this troubled land and live out his days in a less menacing atmosphere. The other factor that operated against the Negro church was its consuming concern with the salvation of souls, the readying of men for full and total adjustment in the world beyond the grave. Like its white counterpart, the Negro church neglected the social ethic, was unconcerned about where men would live, what they would eat, and how they would clothe themselves on this side of the Jordan.

Meanwhile, the nation lunged from slavery through Reconstruction into the race riots of the early 1900s. White attitudes hardened, segregation signs sprouted over every bathroom and drinking fountain, in every railroad train and bus, and the white segregationist invoked the name of God to justify his lynchings, police brutality, injustice before the law, as well as the denial of every right the Constitution had given to the Negro.

Negro churchmen realized the situation was getting grave. A young theologian, Benjamin E. Mays, now President of Morehouse College, and one of the three American official mourners at the funeral of Pope John XXIII, wrote his doctoral thesis on the Negroes' God. That was almost forty years ago, and even then Dr. Mays suspected that the Negroes' religion had better take on more militancy and that this militancy should be rooted in some kind of God concept.

At the end of World War II American Negro soldiers—so movingly described in John Oliver Killens' novel *And Then We Heard the Thunder*—came home determined to do something about their own society. The children of these soldiers are now marching the streets of Birmingham, Jackson, and New York City. They were spawned by the same era that produced Malcolm X and comedian Dick Gregory, both of whom are part and parcel of the same movement. It is not coincidental that the freedom riders and Malcolm X came upon the scene at the same time. They both emerged from a growing Negro consensus that old paths have led nowhere, that they lead the wandering Negro around and around the foot of the mountain but never lead him on toward his goal.

The Peddler of Silks and Scripture

Nineteen-thirty was the year after the big crash on Wall Street. For the Negro in Detroit the crash had a double meaning. It not only meant that he would be unemployed, that there would be no money, but that the subtle discrimination of the North—the very thing that had caused him to leave the South—would become bold and overt. Into the Negro ghetto of Detroit, late in the summer of 1930, there came a peddler, a man of unknown origin and lineage, who sold silks and satins from door to door. He was a strange-looking man. Because of his pale yellow coloring, some thought he was an Arab, others thought he was a Palestinian, and others felt that he had come from India. He called himself W. D. Fard on most occasions. Other times he was variously known as Mr. Farrad Mohammad, Mr. F. M. Ali, Professor Ford, and Mr. Wali Farrad. One of his Detroit followers quotes him as having said, "My name is W. D. Fard, and I come from the Holy City of Mecca. More about myself I will not tell you yet, for the time is not yet come. I am your brother. You have not yet seen me in my royal robes."

There are no documented facts as to just who Fard was or where he came from. However, he found easy entry into

the homes of lower-class Detroit Negroes, who were eager to purchase the silks he claimed were like those worn by black men in Africa.

Dr. Eric Lincoln has gathered information showing that Fard also used his presence in Negro homes to spread a curious doctrine which, in Lincoln's words, found anxious ears "among culture-hungry Negroes." The evidence suggests that Fard mixed the peddling of silks with lectures on the black man's past. He became known as "The Prophet" and concentrated his teachings on his experience in the Near and Far East.

Fard often warned his listeners against certain foods and drinks. ". . . he would eat whatever we had on the table," one of his followers said, "but after the meal he began to talk. 'Now don't eat this food, it is poison for you. The people in your own country do not eat it. Since they eat the right kind of food they have the best health always. If you would just live like the people in your home country, you would not be sick any more.' So we all wanted him to tell us about ourselves and about our home country and about how we could be free from rheumatism, aches, and pains."

Fard was also well versed in the Bible and he used it as a textbook while, at the same time, advising Negroes to renounce Christianity. Realizing that the Bible was the only religious literature known to the Negro, Fard skillfully used it to support his version of the black man's history and the white man's destiny. In the beginning Fard peddled his wares by day and held house meetings at night. But as the Depression deepened and his attack upon the white man grew more bitter, the crowds overflowed the small living rooms and dining rooms of the Detroit slum area. The followers of Fard hired a hall, which they named The Temple of Islam. And that was the birth of the phenomenon known today as the Black Muslims. Fard seems to have been a very friendly, relaxed man with an intuitive mastery of mass psychology. His attacks on members of the white race and on the Bible shocked his listeners into ecstasy and many became converts to his amazing brand of Islam.

"Up to that day I always went to the Baptist Church," one convert said. "After I heard the sermon from the prophet, I was turned around completely. When I went home and

heard that dinner was ready, I said, 'I don't want to eat, I just want to go back to the meeting.' "

It was inevitable that legends would pop up about a man like W. D. Fard. Eric Lincoln has gathered and reported them as follows:

One such legend is that Fard was a Jamaican Negro whose father was a Syrian Moslem. Another describes him as a Palestinian Arab who had participated in various racial agitations in India, South Africa and London before moving on to Detroit. Some of his followers believed him to be the son of wealthy parents of the tribe of Koreish—the tribe of Mohammed, founder of classical Islam. Others say that he was educated at London University in preparation for a diplomatic career in the service of the Kingdom of Hejaz, but that he sacrificed his personal future "to bring 'freedom, justice, and equality' to the 'black men in the wilderness of North America, surrounded and robbed completely by the Cave Man.'" Fard announced himself to the Detroit police as "the Supreme Ruler of the Universe," and at least some of his followers seem to have considered him divine. At the other extreme, a Chicago newspaper investigating the Black Muslim Movement refers to Fard as "a Turkish-born Nazi agent [who] worked for Hitler in World War II."

As for Fard himself, he said that he had been sent to alert the black people of America to the unlimited possibilities of the universal black man in a world now usurped, but temporarily so, by white "blue-eyed devils." This teaching was a sweet shock to illiterate Negroes whose lives had been spent in fear of the white man. They were irresistibly attracted to a black man who would stand tall, call the white man a snake, a devil—a blue-eyed devil, at that—and predict that his reign over the world would soon come to an ignominious end. And when Fard taught that the white man was full of tricks, always to be suspected, never to be trusted, the Southern Negroes who had come to Detroit in search of freedom only to find futility could not resist the temptation to shout "Amen." As Eric Lincoln says, "The North was no promised land: It was the South all over

again with the worst features of racial prejudice thinly camouflaged by sweet talk about equality."

The black Detroiters who heard Fard were starving, living in overcrowded slums. They were the victims of police brutality, the continuing symbol of the power of the white establishment. They were bitter toward the white workers who took over "Negro jobs" as work became more scarce. Even the white welfare workers in Detroit, according to Eric Lincoln, deliberately abused Negroes by making them wait long hours in line before passing out pitiful supplies of flour and lard. All this fear resulted in deep resentment and despair. The words of Fard began to make more sense than ever.

Once Fard had secured a temple, the frequency of his meetings was stepped up and the movement became more formalized. Prospective members were put through rigid examinations and were called upon to make commitments and pledges. The sermons at Fard's meetings were always based on the same subject: the untrustworthiness of the white man and the need for the Negro to understand and return to his glorious history in Africa and Asia.

Eric Lincoln says that Fard, with no literature or material to espouse his cause, used the writings of Joseph F. "Judge" Rutherford, then leader of Jehovah's Witnesses; Van Loon's *Story of Mankind;* Breasted's *The Conquest of Civilization;* the Quran; the Bible; and certain literature of Freemasonry, to bring his people to "knowledge of self." The followers of Fard were encouraged to buy radios so that they could hear the expressions of Rutherford and Frank Norris, the Baptist fundamentalist preacher.

Once temple meetings began, however, Fard told his members that the words of any white man could not be trusted, for the white man was incapable of telling the truth. He insisted that the white man's writings were filled with a symbolism that must be interpreted. Fard went on to establish himself as the interpreter and brought the throng to its feet cheering when he said that the stupid white man was actually a tool in the hands of Allah, that the white man was a dumb idiot who unknowingly told the "truth" and thus predicted his own doom. Fard himself gave the movement its two basic theological pieces: *The Sacred Ritual of the Nation of Islam,* still the key docu-

ment for the Black Muslims, and *Teachings for the Lost Found Nation of Islam in a Mathematical Way,* a religious cryptogram distributed among Muslims but which only Fard could interpret.

Within four years after he had set up the first temple, Fard, who turned out to be an extremely able executive, not only had a burgeoning membership of followers, but had founded a University of Islam, a combination of elementary and high-school education devoted to higher mathematics, astronomy, and the "ending of the spook civilization." To augment all this, Fard established "The Muslim Girls Training Class" to drill Muslim women in the art of being good housewives and mothers. And to put down any trouble with unbelievers and police, he organized "The Fruit of Islam," a quasi-military organization in which men were divided into squads headed by captains and taught the tactics of judo and the use of firearms. Completing the temple structure, a minister was appointed by Fard to run the entire organization.

The Man from Sandersville

One of Fard's Detroit converts was Elijah Poole, a Negro from Sandersville, Georgia, and the son of a Baptist minister. Poole was born on October 7, 1897, one of the thirteen children of Wali and Marie Poole, both of whom had been slaves. After completing the fourth grade—he was then sixteen years old—Poole left home. In 1923 he and his wife, Clara Evans, along with their two children moved to Detroit. Of all the disenchanted Detroit Negroes, Elijah Poole was probably the bitterest. The lure of Detroit had proved a nightmare; he worked in factories at several different jobs until the Depression hit in 1929. In 1930 Poole attended one of the house meetings and heard Fard; in Poole's words, Fard took him "out of the gutters in the streets of Detroit and taught me knowledge of Islam."

Almost from the onset Fard and Poole seemed to become fast friends. Early members of the sect have stated that Elijah Poole became something of an errand boy for Fard

and also helped him publish a newspaper. The key fact in the relationship between Elijah Poole and Fard was *time*. Poole came into the movement at the moment police in Detroit were breathing down Fard's neck. Indeed it was fear of trouble from the police—and nonbelievers—that caused Fard to organize The Fruit of Islam. The same concern caused Fard to organize his temple in such a manner that he would seldom risk public exposure. Once Fard had fashioned his tightly knit organization he appointed a Chief Minister of Islam to preside over the entire movement.

Elijah Poole was tapped by Fard as the first Chief Minister of Islam and given the coveted "original name" *Muhammad*. Earlier in 1932, three years after he joined the movement, Elijah Muhammad went to Chicago and established what has since become known as Temple Number Two, which is now the headquarters of the Black Muslim movement. Trouble in Detroit, however, seems to have cut short Muhammad's sojourn in Chicago. The history of this period is clouded by controversy, but the following is the best sequence of events observers have been able to piece together:

Shortly after (perhaps before) Elijah Muhammad left Detroit for Chicago one of the Muslim brothers got into trouble with the Detroit police because of his alleged part in the sacrificial killing of a fellow Muslim. It is a matter of record that the Muslims did teach sacrificial killing at that time and that Fard was arrested in connection with the charge. Muhammad has written of the incident in these words:

> He was persecuted, sent to jail in 1932, and ordered out of Detroit, Michigan, May 26, 1933. He came to Chicago in the same year, was arrested almost immediately, and placed behind prison bars. He submitted himself with all humility to his persecutors. Each time he was arrested he sent for me that I may see and learn the price of truth for us (the so-called Negroes).

Muhammad gave Fard refuge in Chicago. Shortly thereafter Elijah was named Fard's first Minister of Islam and returned to Detroit, where he took over the movement despite opposition from several of Fard's followers. Shaken by his encounter with police, Fard withdrew from public view,

leaving Elijah Muhammad to stand as the public presence for the movement. During 1933 Fard was seen less and less; then, in 1934, he simply vanished. To this writing, state and federal authorities have been unable to solve the riddle of Fard's disappearance. As Eric Lincoln says, "All reports about the whereabouts of Fard wind up at a dead end." The report that he was seen aboard a ship bound for Europe was never substantiated. The report that he met foul play at the hands of Detroit police or some of his dissident friends was never confirmed. And the dark hint that Elijah Muhammad himself was in some way connected with Fard's disappearance has not been supported by any evidence.

Although rumors persist to this day that Muhammad induced Fard to offer himself up as a human sacrifice, there is no evidence to support them. Yet as Eric Lincoln comments, "It is interesting to note that Fard is honored by [Black] Muslims everywhere as the 'Saviour' and is celebrated as such every year on his birthday, February 26."

Once Fard fell from view, Muhammad became leader of the movement. He was able to bring many dissidents back into the temple, but soon broke with the Detroit faction and returned to Chicago to set up his headquarters. Muhammad had learned church administration from his clergyman father and was able to organize several new temples of Islam. Fard was apotheosized and referred to as the Prophet of Allah; Muhammad proclaimed himself the Messenger of the Prophet of Allah. To this day, the wellspring of Muhammad's power flows from the fact that he was with Fard in life and possibly in death. On one occasion he said, "I have it from the mouth of God that the enemy had better try to protect my life and see that I continue to live. Because if anything happens to me, I will be the last one that they murder. And if any of my followers are harmed, ten of the enemy's best ones will be killed."

Fard and Muhammad shared an affinity for getting into trouble with the law. In 1934 Muhammad refused to transfer his children from the University of Islam to another, accredited school, and he was convicted of contributing to the delinquency of a minor and placed on six months' probation. Eight years later the Messenger was arrested by federal authorities, convicted of refusing to register for the draft, and sentenced to four years in the federal prison at

Milan, Michigan. The indictment, however, alleged that Muhammad taught Negroes that their interests were in a Japanese victory in World War II, since Negroes were ethnic brothers of the Japanese. Muhammad's pro-Japanese sentiments were probably influenced by Japanese efforts, principally through a skilled operative named Major Takahashi who was in Chicago around 1938, to proselytize among the Muslims and other Negro groups. Rank-and-file Muslims, however, showed little interest in Takahashi's propaganda, just as they had shown little interest in Communist overtures in 1932.

Like other men with a messianic complex, Muhammad seemed to grow both in stature and spirit behind bars. First of all, he was clearly able to direct the movement even while he was in prison, and once he was released, he began uttering statements that made Fard and, indeed, the early Elijah Muhammad sound conservative. In bold staccato phrases, punctuated by clearing of the throat so endemic to Southern Negro preachers, Muhammad shouted to the throng that the white man is a snake, a devil by nature, evil, incapable of doing right. Despite the fact that he was still garbed in his "release suit," Muhammad told the Chicago crowd that it made no sense for Negroes in this country to have fought against the Japanese, who were victimized by the same blue-eyed devil who had victimized the American Negro. But Muhammad did not stop there; he said that the American Negro had had no stake in World War II. "Rather," Muhammad said, "the American Negro should be saving his energy and ammunition for 'The Battle of Armageddon,' which will be waged in the wilderness of North America. This battle—and this is one of the central teachings of the Nation of Islam—will be for freedom, justice, and equality. It will be waged to success or under death." Muhammad always titillates his followers by telling them that he cannot at this moment let them know just when the battle will take place and who the protagonists will be. But one has only to sit in the audience and hear his followers applaud and laugh to know that they fully believe that the time of the bloodletting is nigh and that the struggle will be between black and white.

Despite his boldness, the movement stagnated under Muhammad's leadership. In the mid-forties "The Big X" came

on the scene. And with the arrival of Malcolm Little—christened into Islam Malcolm X and elevated by Elijah Muhammad to be Malcolm Shabazz, but known to the pimps, prostitutes, and dope addicts as "Big Red"—the Black Muslim movement really began to move.

Big Red

Malcolm Little was born in Omaha, Nebraska, in 1925, and like Elijah Muhammad he was the son of a Baptist minister. The family soon moved from Omaha to Lansing, Michigan. Malcolm's father was a follower of the Black Nationalist, Marcus Garvey, who felt that all Negroes should return to Africa and escape the oppression of the white man. The Ku Klux Klan burned down the family home when Malcolm was only six years old. "The firemen came," Malcolm says, "and just sat there without making any effort to put one drop of water on the fire. The same fire that burned my father's home still burns in my soul."

Following Garvey's teaching that the Negroes should go into business, Mr. Little then set out to build his own store. Soon after this, according to Malcolm, "my father was found with his head bashed and his body mangled under a streetcar." Malcolm Shabazz to this day remains convinced that his father was lynched by white people who resented even the prospect of a Negro gaining some economic independence. With his father's death, Malcolm's family was forced to separate. In moving terms, clenching his fists, and at times breaking into tears, Malcolm has described to me how his mother boiled dandelion greens from day to day trying to keep her eleven children from starving to death. "We stayed dizzy and sick because we stayed hungry." At night Malcolm and his brothers would go out and steal what food they could to fill their stomachs. The Littles were a clannish bunch. They struggled to stay together, but the pangs of hunger were too great, and they were ripped apart. Malcolm was sent to an institution for boys.

This turned out to be the second molding factor in the life of Malcolm X. He was one of the few Negroes—if not

the only one—in the institution and he developed a warm love for the white matron who defended him when other kids were "kicking him around." In the only complimentary statement I have heard him make about a white person, Malcolm says of the matron, "She was good to me. I followed her around like a little puppy. I was a kind of mascot." She arranged for him to attend a near-by school where, although he was the only Negro pupil, his keen mind put him at the head of the class, which only gained him the resentment of both the teacher and the pupils.

"When I was in the eighth grade," Malcolm says, "they asked me what I wanted to become. I told them I wanted to study law. But they told me that law was not a suitable profession for a Negro. They suggested that I think of a trade such as carpentry."

That ripped it! Malcolm soon left school and came east to New York, and in a matter of weeks penetrated the underworld where he became a trusted lieutenant. Malcolm's early days in the underworld are described in unpublished notes by writer Alex Haley in the following words:

Admitted to the underworld's fringes, sixteen-year-old Malcolm absorbed all he heard and saw. He swiftly built up a reputation for honesty by turning over every dollar due his boss ("I have always been intensely loyal"). By the age of 18, Malcolm was versatile "Big Red." He hired from four to six men variously plying dope, numbers, bootleg whiskey and diverse forms of hustling. Malcolm personally squired well-heeled white thrill-seekers to Harlem sin dens, and Negroes to white sin downtown. "My best customers were preachers and social leaders, police and all kinds of big shots in the business of controlling other people's lives."

His income often reached as high as two thousand dollars a month. And I have heard Malcolm talk of paying off the cops from a thousand-dollar bankroll which he pulled from the pocket of his two-hundred-dollar suit. But not even "Big Red" had enough money to pay all of the policemen and eventually Malcolm X went to prison for burglary.

It was in 1947, in the maximum security prison at Concord, Massachusetts, that Malcolm was converted to the

teachings of The Honorable Elijah Muhammad by one of his fellow prisoners who was a member of the Detroit temple. From that moment Malcolm has neither smoked, cursed, drunk, nor run after women. He is the most puritanical man I have ever met. I have interviewed him scores of times but he will not meet me for an interview at any place where liquor is sold. He does not object to my smoking, but in polite terms he makes it understood that he would rather I didn't smoke around him. I have entertained him in my home along with other guests, and he has sat relaxed on the floor as we drink. He has never taken anything but coffee, although he knows full well that none of us would ever betray him.

Indeed, it is around the widely known and deeply admired morality of Malcolm X that one of the few pieces of humor about the Muslim movement came into being.

The story is that Malcolm was attempting to convert a Negro Baptist to the teaching of Islam.

"What are the rules of your organization?" the Negro asked.

"Well," Malcolm said, "my brother, you have to stop drinking, stop swearing, stop gambling, stop using dope, and stop cheating on your wife!"

"Hell," the convert replied, "I think I had better remain a Christian."

3. THE NATION
OF ISLAM

Any objective evaluation of the Black Muslims as a religious body must begin with a fresh look at religion itself, its origin and meaning. The current, widespread antipathy toward the Black Muslims makes such a basic review of the roots of religion all the more necessary. Above all we must shut out the voices of those who insist that the Black Muslims are not a religion because they—the critics—don't like what the Muslims preach and do. After all, the Mormon Church holds, among other things, that the Negro is inferior because he is the descendant of Ham, the accursed son of Noah. As a result Negroes are allowed to join the Mormon Church, but are barred from high church office. But none of us will take the position that the Mormons are not a religion.

To understand the Black Muslims—and the Mormons, for that matter—we must retrace that contorted and tribal path man and God have walked together en route to the here and now.

Religion as a Group Experience

The world has always been a mystery to man. It excites his imagination, challenges his courage, and piques his intellect. But the individual never meets the world alone. He is of his group; the group is part of the world he inherited on the day he discovered himself and the other members of his group—like the thunder and the lightning and the sun and the trees and the rivers and the canyons and

the hurricanes and the manna trees that are part of that which confounds him. Collectively confounded, then, the group members react as one. They create a god almost always in their own image and attribute to him all of the omnipotence and omnipresence required to account for a plot of matter spinning dizzily through space into nowhere. And if he is in their image, then he is their father and they are his children. He watches over them and protects them from the pestilences that come by day and the evils that crawl by night. They are his chosen people and he walks with the warriors of the tribe as they go forth to battle temporal evil, which is to say, anything and anybody that differs from their tribe.

In return, the tribesmen insist that god make demands upon them. And god grants their request: He commands them to bow down and worship him, and to put no other god before him. He commands them to love one another even as they love him and he loves them. His commandments on social ethics always parallel the social history of the tribe involved. If one day some members of the tribe feel sick from having eaten the meat from a given animal, then god decrees that such meat is unclean and that it is sinful to eat of it. If the social history of the people discloses that the affinity between the man and his woman is so intense that the intrusion of any other man or woman upon that relationship brings on community disorder, then god decrees that a man shall have one wife and a woman one husband, and then commands that the neighbors covet not the man's wife or the woman's husband. And when the tribe matures to the point of having old men, elders, steeped in the history of the tradition of the people, god orders that the aged be respected and all be venerated as his leaders on earth.

Thus it is that the god of a tribe becomes "their" god. History is replete with battle scars left when the gods of an opposing people fought it out on the plains and in the valleys. When tribe meets tribe in war, at least one of the tribes is bound to lose. But even in defeat the god of the tribe becomes more powerful than ever before as the tribe is convinced that, though it has lost a battle, it will eventually win the war. Thus, in the words of one of the great

tribal leaders, "Our god is able to deliver. But if not, we will not bow down and serve your god."

Although tribal life revolves around the god concept, few tribal states have actually become theocracies. Religious leaders have taken their place beside temporal leaders, and they function in concord, under the umbrella of their god to make the state a practical institution.

With the dawn of modern history, gods began to fuse and merge as people began to widen the circle of their experience and accept the reality of tribal pluralism, and civilizations that have survived to matter in the context of the current world are those that fly the banner of the world's four or five major religions.

Modern man knows little of all this because he inherited already thought-out religions. Thus he has no idea how primitive and crude his gods once were. And it is precisely because of modern man's religious sophistication that the Black Muslims rasp: At stage center, and before an audience that is weary of racism and religious bigotry, the all-black Nation of Islam gleefully re-enacts the shoddy scenes of our cultural beginnings.

"We are in the image of God," Malcolm says.

"Make it plain, Brother Minister. Make it plain."

"That means that God—we call him Allah—must be black like me!"

"All praise due to Allah."

"God was here in the beginning."

"Yes sir, that's right."

"So we were here from the beginning"—and Malcolm X smiles.

The people come roaring to their feet with shouts of thanks and deliverance.

"And that which was here from the beginning must be the daddy of everything else. Am I right or wrong?"

"You right. That's right."

"This blue-eyed devil talking about he is superior. It's about time he found out that we are his pappy!"

"Make it plain, Brother. Make it plain."

"Now listen to this," Malcolm told a rally of three thousand on a Harlem street corner, "and you will know why black is superior."

"Come on. Come, let's hear it!"

"Black is *the* prime color. It is the strong color."

"Yes!"

"You can get any other color you want by mixing colors, but you cannot find colors that you can mix and produce black. Only black can produce black."

"Make it plain."

"And if black is prime, that means it is God, that means it is good."

"That's right!"

"Therefore the less black you are the less good you are."

"All praise due to Allah." And now the people sense the great truth that is about to come, and they begin to break with laughter.

"Therefore when you are white, you are as nonblack as you can be."

"Make it plain, Malcolm. Make it plain."

"Therefore when you are white you are absolutely nongood; am I right or wrong?"

"You right!"

"In other words," Malcolm shouts, "the white man is therefore absolutely evil, a snake and a devil, and his time of destruction draws nigh!"

With this the crowd breaks with joy. The applause lasts for several minutes; white policemen standing guard at the meeting nudge white onlookers, telling them to "move on."

This argument, that God is black and the white man a devil, presents the Black Muslims with the identical philosophical dilemma that has plagued most religions: How could a good (black) God create a bad (white) thing?

The doctrine concerning Yakub is the Black Muslims' attempt to answer that riddle. In biological terms of reference, accepting the Muslim notion that the black man is the original man, they must explain how the black race produced white people. Elijah Muhammad states the argument in these terms: The Caucasian race was created out of the weak of the black race; they are the handiwork of Yakub, a black scientist who rebelled against Allah. Dr. Eric Lincoln is correct when he says that the doctrine of Yakub is the central myth of the Black Muslim movement. But it is also the tenet the Black Muslims seem to know least about.

Writing in the *Pittsburgh Courier*, Elijah Muhammad detailed in these words the mechanics by which the black scientist Yakub made the white man:

> Who are the white race? I have repeatedly answered that question in this [column] for nearly the past three years. "Why are they white-skinned?" Answer: Allah (God) said this is due to being grafted from the Original Black Nation, as the Black Man has two germs (two people) in him. One is black and the other brown. The brown germ is weaker than the black germ. The brown germ can be grafted into its last stage, and the last stage is white. A scientist by the name of Yakub discovered this knowledge . . . 6,645 years ago, and was successful in doing this job of grafting after 600 years of following a strict and rigid birth control law.

According to Elijah Muhammad the experiment was a success, but it also resulted in the "blue-eyed devils" who now people the world and have low physical and moral stamina. Muhammad then goes on to show the physical superiority of the black man by underlining the victories of Negro ballplayers and prize fighters. He then points up what he calls the low morality of the white man by citing the gas chambers of Germany, the atomic bomb of Hiroshima, and all the abuses white Southerners (and Northerners) have heaped upon the Negro.

Summing up the results of Yakub's experiment, Elijah Muhammad issues this finding:

> The human beast—the serpent, the dragon, the devil, and Satan—all mean one and the same: the people or race known as the white or Caucasian race, sometimes called the European race.
>
> Since by nature they were created liars and murderers, they are the enemies of truth and righteousness, and the enemies of those who seek the truth. . . .

But their certification of the white man as a devil, one incapable of doing good, rests on more than metaphysical grounds. It involves history. To make their historical point the Black Muslims part company with the established world

historians. They begin their argument by establishing—with some accuracy—that the black man in Africa had a developed civilization at the time that, in Malcolm's words, "the white savages of Europe were living in caves and crawling around on their all-fours." It was the intrusion of the white man into Africa that spoiled things and brought slavery to the New World.

The decline of the black man in Africa is only temporary. The white devil was given about six thousand years to flaunt his evil and then he was to be destroyed as the black man returned to power. The white man's time ran out just as World War I was raging; the Black Muslims overcame the fact that this was an excellent time for the prophecy to come true—after all, white people were out to destroy each other—with the argument that sets the American stage for the followers of The Honorable Elijah Muhammad.

The only reason the destruction of the white man didn't come off on schedule, according to the Muslims, is that so many black men are all mixed up with the white, that it is impossible to destroy the evil men without destroying some "originals," that is to say, Negroes. This, then, is what Muhammad and Malcolm are talking about when they speak to "the lost-found black man in the wilderness of North America." They are really saying that the restoration of black men to world power is being delayed because of the American Negro; the white man has been given a new dispensation, actually, not because he deserves it but to give the Negro time to separate from those scheduled for destruction.

Herein lies the reasoning behind Muhammad's talk about a separate state; this is why the Black Muslims with their tremendous power over people are unable to participate in any of the current civil-rights actions; they can't help but fight for better jobs, better schools, or better housing. They are committed to getting out from among the white man as soon as possible, lest they share his doom of the fire, which is sure not only to come next time, but to come soon.

To plug up the logical and emotional leaks in such an argument as this, the Black Muslims must propagate a continuously expanding "line." They must maintain the "Islamic" tinge but at the same time keep their teaching within American terms of reference that Negroes can understand;

they must take Negroes who have a struggle with English and teach them Arabic; they must convince the most Western of men that they are Arabs.

This cultural island-hopping can backfire, sometimes with amusing results. I attended a Black Muslim bazaar with writer Alex Haley. Elijah Muhammad was scheduled to appear but sent his son, Akbar, instead. Akbar, a slender, dark-brown twenty-five-year-old, came before the crowd of some two thousand garbed in a flowing white sheet. In Middle Eastern Arabic circles Akbar would have been considered in his Sunday best, but to Harlem Negroes Akbar's dress smacked of the Ku Klux Klan, hardly an image one wishes to raise in a man he hopes to convert. Yet this is the cross-cultural problem the Black Muslims must continually deal with.

I have seen Malcolm X do this with tremendous effectiveness. I once debated with him on TV in Los Angeles. He took the stand of a Muslim, saying that the Moslem faith was the black man's original culture. Malcolm must make this basic thrust or all else he says rests on historical sand. As we were leaving the studio, we were greeted by several white students, Moslems from Persia, who complained to Malcolm that they had attempted to visit Muhammad's temples and were refused entry because they were white blue-eyed devils. Malcolm glossed the matter over, and they all parted wishing Allah's blessing each upon the other. In reality, Malcolm is not interested in any white people, Moslem or not. These Persians could no more get in a Black Muslim temple than Governor Faubus could. "Let's look at it this way," Malcolm told the Persians. "If a lion is in a cage, his roar will be different from the roar of the lion who is in the forest. That," he concluded, "is why you couldn't get in our temple. But both the lion in the forest and the lion in the cage are lions. That is what matters. Lions love lions; they hate leopards."

Translated, Malcolm was saying that the American Negro, as a Moslem, must make different noises from the free Moslems of, say, Persia, because the American Negro is in a cage. The cage, of course, is white civilization; that is why the roar of the American Negro Moslem is so provincial; that is why Persians would do well to worship Allah in their own way in their own temples, while the

Black Muslims and Allah have their rendezvous in a dinky auditorium over a pool hall in Los Angeles' Negro ghetto.

It is in such meetings that Malcolm adds the historical ingredient to his theology. It takes two forms:

First, the Black Muslims excite Negroes to shouts by proving that the Negro is somebody, a man with a past and a history. I know from personal experience that Malcolm X is one of the best-versed people in America on African history. I have sat with him in private and general gatherings where he has recited startling facts about the nature of early African civilizations. When challenged, Malcolm is always able to produce a text—and a legitimate one at that —to support what he says. Malcolm's teachings come as a surprise not because they are new, previously unknown facts about Africa, but because the entire system of education in the Western World, particularly in America, has carefully distorted the true history of Africa to support the notion of white, male supremacy. And so it is from Malcolm X, not from his sixth-grade history teacher—who is probably white—that the Negro child in the North learns the truth about Africa and what once really happened there.

The second historical aspect of the Muslim doctrine involves an intensive study of the role of the American Negro in American history. Here again Malcolm and his followers walk into a void left by the American education system. The black child in Harlem learns about the Revolutionary War but he does not learn that the man who set it off by leading the Americans in the Boston Massacre was a Negro, Crispus Attucks. The black child sees the clock work but he does not know that Benjamin Bannaker, a Negro, invented the pendulum. The black child visits the blood bank but he does not know that a Negro, Dr. Charles Drew, discovered how to preserve blood and thus made the bank possible. Nobody tells the Negro child these things in school. On the contrary, the child is taught that American civilization flowed, for the most part, from white brains. And when Malcolm, to use his words, "pulls the cover off the white devil and tells black men the truth about the work of their ancestors," the Negro child shrieks with pride and joy—probably for the first time in his life.

Malcolm X brings his message of importance and dignity to a class of Negroes who have had little, if any, reason to

feel proud of themselves as a race or as individuals. Their encounters with white people are always unpleasant situations in which Negroes find themselves embarrassed or emasculated. Think it out for yourself: What contact does the Negro in Harlem have with the white man?

The white man is the *man* they must meet every morning when they go to work in the garment district; the *man* they must meet when the rent is due; the *man* they face when they go to the pawnshop; the *man* who comes and sells things on credit; the *man* who buys the installment paper and comes to collect the payments; the *man* who gets work when they cannot; the *man* whom they see on TV loosing dogs on Negro children; the *man* they face as a schoolteacher who does not understand them and who is often contemptuous of them—the man, the man, the man, the white man, the goddam white man! And when Malcolm X says the white man is a devil, they roar "amen" because every experience they have with a white man is a devilish one.

Chilling though it may be, the Black Muslims have erected their teaching on a group experience common to all American Negroes. Few of us concur in their conviction and sentencing of the white race. But none of us can question the accuracy of the indictment on which that conviction rests.

Elijah Goes to Mecca

The *hajj*, the long, dusty pilgrimage to Mecca that every Moslem looks forward to, is the final criterion of whether one is or is not a Moslem. Only certified followers of Islam are allowed to enter Mecca during the holy period of the pilgrimage.

"Elijah Muhammad is not a Moslem," said Imam Talib Ahmad Dawud in 1960. "He is just plain Elijah Poole of Sandersville, Georgia." Dawud, an American Negro and leader of the Muslim Brotherhood USA, was then locked in a bitter struggle with the Black Muslims over the question of their religious authenticity. But the Imam's remarks couldn't have been more ill-timed. Even as Dawud was

denouncing the Black Muslims, Elijah was packing his bags
for a trip "back home where I can visit and pray with my
own people." Several days after he departed from New York,
Elijah placed his credentials before the eagle-eyed *hajj* committee, the final judge of who may march to Mecca and
pray. Elijah Muhammad was admitted without delay, and
Black Muslims—the word was cabled back and came over
the wire services—held meetings of praise and thanks all
over the nation.

That was that. Muhammad was admitted to the *hajj,* he
made the holy walk to Mecca. Who, then, is to dispute his
religious credentials?

Muhammad's journey to Mecca brought an end to all the
arguments about his true affiliation with traditional Islam.
When Mike Wallace and I were preparing a TV docu-
mentary on the Black Muslims, the orthodox Moslems denounced the movement. "They teach race hate," one Islamic
spokesman told us, "and that means they couldn't be Moslems." The Federation of Islamic Associations of Chicago is
the official Moslem organization in the United States and
Canada. They have denounced Elijah; they have praised
him for conducting the largest Arabic school in America
and for accepting the Koran as law, but federation officials
are "suspicious" of him. These Moslems, however, are largely
of European descent, although their ranks are peppered with
a few Negro converts. Their rejection of Elijah rests on
his argument concerning racism, and they flinch when Muhammad calls himself "The Messenger of Allah."

Rejection from such a group is grist for the Black Muslims' mill. Malcolm X holds them up to high ridicule and
scorn, saying they have been corrupted by Christianity and
that they look very much like "the blue-eyed devil who enslaved us and took away our culture." In his "University
Speech" (see Part Two of this book) Malcolm rains fire
upon these "European Moslems" who have "passed us by
in an attempt to make our slave masters Moslems."

There are several clear differences between Black Muslims and orthodox Moslems. Whether these differences read
Elijah and his followers out of the Islamic brotherhood is
a matter to be determined by Islamic officials. These are
some of the differences between the two groups:

—The Black Muslims will not allow white persons in

their temples; orthodox Moslems accept worshipers of all races.

—The Black Muslims maintain a separate movement; there seems to be little or no organizational link with the orthodox Moslems. The Black Muslims do not visit the orthodox Moslem temples, and the orthodox Moslems do not come to hear Malcolm X.

—Nowhere in the Koran or in any orthodox Moslem literature is there support for the Black Muslims' teaching about the evil scientist Yakub. Nor is there any support in the teachings of orthodox Moslems to support Elijah's account —see his "Atlanta Speech" in Part Two—that this world was once the moon and was blown up by an evil scientist who wanted to destroy true followers of Allah.

—Orthodox Moslems universally condemn the Black Muslim teaching that the white man is a devil by nature.

—Orthodox Moslems universally object to the Black Muslim preachment concerning a separate state.

But once Muhammad walked into Mecca these differences ceased to matter. To be sure, orthodox Moslems want no part of Elijah and, if pushed, will denounce him. But the *hajj* committee has rendered what must be accepted as the final verdict.

Behind this trip to Mecca lies a typical Black Muslim story. Malcolm X had visited the Near and the Far East the year before. His mission was to make certain key contacts for Muhammad. I followed Malcolm by some several months into Cairo, Egypt, and talked with Moslem officials who had received him with open arms. Malcolm was in Cairo during the holy season, at the very time when thousands of chanting Arabs were wending their way toward Mecca. Malcolm himself was cleared to make the *hajj;* he could have gone to Mecca in 1959 and that would have settled the controversy once and for all. Malcolm elected not to go, not to upstage his teacher and leader. Instead he returned home with the word that all was well in Mecca, that Elijah and his family would be received there with open arms.

The following year, while Malcolm remained at home, Elijah went to Mecca.

Malcolm's ambassadorial work in Cairo—and that is precisely what it was—stunned many of his American detrac-

tors. Others of us who had been close observers of the movement were not surprised. We knew that Malcolm has always maintained excellent relations with top Arabs at the United Nations. Few, if any, of these meetings were ever public. But they did occur and there is every indication that they are still going on. The road to Mecca was cleared long before Malcolm and Elijah left these shores; powerful pro-Nasser Arabs are quietly in Malcolm's corner, and many Black Muslim bazaars open with the reading of cabled greetings from "Our Beloved Brother Gamal Abdel Nasser."

The emphasis of orthodox Islam is universal love and brotherhood among men of all races. The central teaching of the Black Muslims is that all white men are devils and will soon be destroyed. It seems superfluous to point out the wide disparity between these two views. But both Muslim and Moslem worship Allah. And that—at least so the *hajj* committee said—is all that matters.

The answer to this ambiguity, I suspect, lies in the gangling structure of the Moslem hierarchy. Unlike, say, the Catholic Church, the Moslem faith is not a tightly knit, fully administered organization. I have talked with Moslems about all this, and while they would rather that Elijah did not say much of what he says, they are still smarting over the Christian Crusades and readying for the moment of truth with the Jews. The Black Muslims carefully describe themselves as "anti-Zionist" rather than as against the Jews. But herein, I suspect, is the resolution of the entire matter of Elijah's relationship to orthodox Islam.

A high Islamic official in Cairo explained it to me in these words: "Of course your Black Muslims are improperly informed. But they are turning men to Allah, away from Christianity, toward Mecca. This is what we want; this is what we must have. We need new blood in western Islam. If Muhammad can give that new blood we welcome him. As for his teachings," the official continued, "we will see to it that the correct view is given to the black man in America. Now the thing is to get them facing toward Mecca."

Is This a True Religion?

Although Elijah has made his holy pilgrimage to Mecca, the debate over the religious validity of the Black Muslims still rages, with the movement's critics holding to their charge that Elijah Muhammad teaches hate whereas true religion teaches love. A case can be made that these critics are doubly in error, first in their assumption that their own faith teaches universal love, and secondly in their conclusion—aided by news accounts—that the Black Muslims actually preach hatred of others.

Every religion is a closed network of believers; it has its dogma, its ritual, its gods. The followers of that faith are taught to love one another and are urged to proselytize sinners (outsiders) wherever they can be found. Most religions draw creedal, not racial, lines. Persons of any race may embrace the tenets of the faith and become members. However, this is not always the case and racial overtones have crept into major world faiths.

The late, and loved, Pope John flirted with immortality by coming to grips with the issue of racism in religion. Not only did he infuse the Church with the fresh air of universalism, but he halted a service because a priest violated —forgot, actually—His Holiness' order that a reference to the Jews as a "perfidious people" be stricken from the Catholic prayer service. The pending second session of the ecumenical council may see the introduction of a proposal that would call on the Church to speak out against anti-Semitism. The proposal was not brought up in the first session because the Church fathers feared what the Arabs might say!

The Jews and the Protestants face essentially the same problems as the Roman Catholics. St. Paul rose to glory because he translated being a Jew from a biological to a spiritual proposition. Many Jews have not accepted that translation and they snicker when Sammy Davis, Jr., walks into their temple. Racism is such a fact of American Protestant church life that most major denominations are divided

along racial lines. Then there is the question of religion and geography. The world's major faiths were spawned in certain areas and took root among people of a common ethnic stock. Thus the followers of Buddha are apt to be Orientals; but for slavery and colonization all of the followers of Christ would be European. But for the same kind of cultural intermingling, Allah's followers would be the peoples of Asia Minor and North Africa, and the black peoples below the Sahara would still be practicing the varied tribal and family faiths mentioned earlier in this essay.

But time and trouble make saints of everybody . . . and universalism occurs only when feuding faiths clash on the plains of practical reality. Thus American Protestants now have a commission that is given over entirely to eliminating all anti-Semitism from the gospel of Christ. The Episcopal Bishop of California, James Pike, has gone so far as to suggest that we take down the cross as a symbol of our faith lest this encourage the teaching that the Jews killed Our Lord. This teaching—that the Jews killed Christ—is no longer fashionable as it was when I was baptized. Now one is told that the Romans killed Christ. And since the once-heathen Romans are now Christians—even though they are Catholics—I suppose this makes things better.

Now let's turn to the other side of the coin.

During a recent lecture before the Jewish Graduate Club at Columbia University I talked about the need for all orthodox religions to relax their dogmas and accept other peoples as equals. One fiercely intent man leaped to his feet and shouted to me, "You want to rob us of our culture because you people don't have one of your own!" This was sheer nonsense and the host rabbi rose to say so. But I pressed the issue: Could I join their temple? The younger Jews shouted "Yes—we would love to have you." The older fellows were not quite so sure.

"Are you as Jews chosen of God, thus the only ones who are really blessed?" I asked one of the fundamentalists.

"Yes," he shot back.

"Are you chosen in a way that I can never be?" I continued.

"Yes." He faltered. "You are not a Jew; you cannot be among the elect."

By this time the younger Jews were on their feet screaming denunciations of him. But the issue of ethnic exclusive-
ness that splits today's Jewish community had been laid bare.

Dogma and ritual are further evidences of the tribalism
endemic to religion. I was born and raised a Baptist;
long before I could read and write I knew that any person
who had not been immersed in water was doomed to Hell.
There was nothing to argue about, no need for polemics
and reasoning; there would be no Methodists in Heaven!

The point of truth is this: Ethnic and dogmatic bigotry
are imbedded in every religious faith plying its wares in
the world market; we religious liberals are sudents of apolo-
getics, sophisticated believers who prefer to forget our crude
and tribalistic roots in favor of an enlightened social ethic.
Alas, along came Elijah and made us see ourselves as we
once were; along came Malcolm X and made us understand
what we are now, and why.

The argument that the Black Muslims are not a valid
religion because of the exclusivity of their fellowship, then,
is clearly spurious. Every religion is a sort of sanctified
country club, a coming together of peers in the name of
their god. The second argument against the religiosity of
the Black Muslims is equally spurious: Like all faiths, the
Black Muslims never say hate the other fellow; they say love
your own kind. Religious bigotry is Western civilization's
major moral blind spot, and Malcolm X has taken up squat-
ters' rights just there.

Thus it is that secularism must save the church—the lay-
man must lead the clergyman to the mourner's bench and
make him confess brotherhood in the name of a democratic
and pluralistic society. The nature of our social moment
demands that we free God from racialism and dogmatics.
Racialism, the malignant one of the two cancers, must be
dealt with first since it is the prime moral issue of our
time. And it must be dealt with by all peoples of all faiths
working in concert. Should our social order change, should
we somehow come to grips with the evils that have spawned
the Black Muslims, the movement would be forced to refine
itself or perish.

Malcolm X is the best authority for this. I have often
pressed him on his categorical denunciation of the white
man as a devil, and his reply is always the same: "The

Honorable Elijah Muhammad teaches us that the white man is a devil. We hold to that teaching because history proves the white man is a devil. If he is not a devil," Malcolm X concludes, "then let him prove it. Let him give justice, freedom, and equality to our people."

I have deliberately kept my analysis of the Black Muslims in personal terms of reference because this is precisely how most Negroes feel about the matter—after all, the attraction of the movement for Negroes is one of the major points of this essay.

"Of course I disagree with Malcolm," the wife of a Negro newsman told me. "But I disagree with a lot of other religions, too. If he teaches hate, so do they; what's the difference? I wonder why the white people are after him." She smiled. "Could it be because he is colored?"

The Black Muslims have their God, their gospel, their ritual trappings, their approval from official heads of the Islamic faith. As a religion, then, there is little left to do but disagree with them and then leave them alone.

This, of course, pains liberals, Negro and white, who want to hear a ringing denunciation of the Black Muslims. Negro leaders are always quick to denounce Elijah, but the Negro masses are strangely silent. There is a reason for this silence, something both the Negro leadership and the white power structure would do well to examine: Deep down in their hearts, as James Baldwin so accurately states, the black masses don't believe in white people any more. They don't believe in Malcolm either, except when he articulates their disbelief in white people. In the end—and this is the thing white people will be a long time in grasping—the Negro masses neither join nor denounce the Black Muslims. They just sit at home in the ghetto amid the heat, the roaches, the rats, the vice, the disgrace, and rue the fact that come daylight they must meet the man—the white man—and work at a job that leads only to a dead end.

This brings me to the core of the matter, to the final measure of every religion: it is a thing called *compassion*, a concern and caring about the other fellow. It is rooted in the glaring awareness that we all have fallen short of the high mark set for us, and thus we need the honest sympathy and understanding of all men everywhere.

For though you may have your God, your holy book,

your ritual, and your symbols; though you may give of
your wages to build the temple; and though you may have
been to Mecca, or Jerusalem, if you have not compassion
you are but meanness couched in Scripture, you are but an
ancient stink, a reason for men to hold their noses as they
crawl on toward a land of human understanding and brotherhood.

The Nation

Once the convert becomes a Black Muslim he is baptized
as a citizen in the Nation of Islam. They have a flag, a
symbol, and a cause. From this day forward his life centers around activity at the Muslim restaurant and temple.

Who are these Black Muslims? Where do they live, and
what do they do for a living?

These questions baffle all observers because any Negro
you encounter could be a Black Muslim. Usually the men
wear identifying pins, and the Muslim women can generally be spotted by their dress, particularly the long, flowing
headpiece. But these identifying signs are not always present.
I have encountered Black Muslims working in printing plants,
in barbershops, as messenger boys, as night-club entertainers,
and as cab drivers. I will never forget taking a stroll in
Central Park where I came across a Muslim sister working as
a nursemaid to three white children! Since most nurses and
maids are Negroes, the rise of the Black Muslims has sent a
quiet but very real chill through the employment agencies in
several major cities. After all, there is no telling what
these Muslim women will do when the "word" comes, when
the Battle of Armageddon is declared. And there is no way
for employment agencies to determine if Negro applicants
are Black Muslims before sending them out as servants in
white homes. Nor is there any way for heads of households
to know just who their butlers and cooks are. To borrow
from James Baldwin, nobody knows their name. It could
be "X."

The Black Muslims flatly refuse to discuss their organizational finances with anyone. However, observers of the

movement are convinced that the tithes collected at temples and the income from temple restaurants form the basis of the Muslim economy. The local restaurant—and most of them are called "Shabazz" restaurants after Malcolm X whose "restored" Arab name is Shabazz—is under the supervision of the local minister. He seems to have fairly complete control, but all matters are subject to review by Malcolm X as Elijah's roving ambassador. The local ministers are allowed a certain portion of what they raise, but only top insiders know just how Mr. Muhammad makes this determination. The major leaders of the movement all seem to have taken a vow of poverty and live on expenses furnished by the movement itself. I know this is true of Malcolm X and I suspect it to be true of others.

But it must be remembered that the Black Muslims are both thrifty and industrious; they are encouraged to open their own businesses and many of the top leaders are themselves businessmen. Elijah Muhammad, Jr., runs one of the largest bakeries in Chicago; Raymond Sharrieff is said to have ownership in a clothing store there. All evidence indicates that local Muslim leaders finance themselves through various enterprises and that the bulk of the funds raised in the temple itself flow on to the movement headquarters in Chicago.

Whoever and wherever these Black Muslims are they lead an exacting, regimented life. In their homes they practice strict dietary laws—precisely those of the kosher Jews—and avoid contact with white people as much as possible. The private role of both the man and the woman in the family is clearly defined, and the children are indoctrinated with the faith while they are still young. Muslim men are watched by The Fruit and must engage in some kind of gainful employment. They are encouraged to go into small business whenever possible; they are assured of patronage from their fellow Muslims. A number of Negro businessmen have been attracted to the Nation of Islam because it provides them with a ready source of customers. Other Muslim brothers can be seen on the streets every day selling Muslim newspapers. They are allowed to keep a goodly portion of what they earn and are thus independent. The temple restaurants employ scores of Muslim men and women, thus decreasing the ranks of their unemployed. Other Muslims are door-to-door

salesmen and find easy entry in the Negro community, where the white door-to-door salesmen have become anathema.

But the average Black Muslim works for some white man somewhere in some capacity. He is urged to learn a trade and thus ready himself for the day when he will be called upon to be one of the heads of industry and commerce in the Muslims' own, separate state.

The Black Muslim men are lectured constantly about family responsibility and are subject to trial before their peers if they violate the rules of the order. Punishment can vary from a small fine to temporary or permanent banishment from the temple. No Muslim will associate with an offender for the duration of his exile. It is said that Malcolm X's brother was once banished and that Malcolm refused even to write the man until the period of punishment had been served.

Black Muslim women are schooled in the art and need for homemaking, and are taught to take a back seat in the presence of their husbands. Muslim women almost never talk to strangers—non-Muslims, that is—and maintain a general silence that is unnerving. They also eschew make-up and fancy dress. When I first encountered the Muslims some five years ago, this ban on feminine adornment was rigidly enforced. But there seems to have been a strong revolt among temple women and the ban has been relaxed to the point where employing make-up is now optional. Yet I have seen few Muslim women exercise this option. The wife of a major Muslim official, say Joseph X of New York, certainly wouldn't exercise it.

The Black Muslims are a male-oriented organization. A man reaches real stature in the movement when he becomes a member of The Fruit of Islam, the functional and disciplinary arm of the movement. The Fruit hold separate temple services, where they are taught, among other things, every possible method of self-defense. Every local temple has a Captain of The Fruit—in New York it is Joseph X— and the entire network is headed by the son-in-law of Elijah Muhammad, Raymond Sharrieff. The Fruit enforce brotherhood among the men of the temple and form the honor guard whenever Malcolm X or Elijah Muhammad makes a public appearance. The Fruit work under the local minister, but there is a line of authority that runs down to the local

captains directly from Sharrieff's Chicago headquarters. The
Muslim Girls Training Class (MGT), for young women, is
headed by Sister Lottie X, also of Chicago.

The division of authority seems to be along these lines:
The local Fruit and MGT work under the local minister
on local matters. But unless the matter in question is one
of clearly defined doctrine the local minister gets clearance
from Chicago before issuing his orders. On national matters, those affecting the movement as a whole, The Fruit
and the MGT take orders directly from headquarters. These
orders are issued to members of the temple who obey without
question.

One of the functions of The Fruit and the MGT is fund-
raising. None of the rumors about Muslims receiving help
from outside—Communist or segregationist—sources has
proved true. The fact of the matter is that the Black Muslims are hard-working, frugal people; they never buy on
installment, and they give a tenth—at least—of their earn-
ings to the temple. This income is augmented by bazaars,
plays, rallies, and the sale of their own newspapers and
magazines. Then there is the matter of the various law-
suits the Muslims have carried on with astonishing success.
The Black Muslims have collected upward of a quarter of
a million dollars I know about in the past four years or so,
mostly as a result of police brutality against their members. These suits are filed in the name of the individual
Muslim but they are carried on by the temple, and I
suspect the temple shares in the results.

Further regimentation of life within the Nation is achieved
by demanding that members send their children to Black
Muslim schools wherever possible. In two cities, Chicago
and Detroit, the Muslims have "universities" where they train
the children from kindergarten through high school. It will
be recalled that Elijah Muhammad first got into trouble with
the law when he decided to send his children to the Muslim
school rather than the public schools. Now authorities in
both cities have approved the Muslim schools as accredited
centers of learning.

These schools are well disciplined and skillfully run.
Early in 1962 there was considerable concern in Chicago
over just what the Black Muslims were teaching in their
schools. A biracial committee visited the University of Islam

there and came away stunned. Said committee member
Judge Edyth Sampson, a former U.S. delegate to the United
Nations, "These people are doing a magnificent job with
their young students. I am deeply impressed by what I saw."

What Mrs. Sampson and her fellow committee members
saw was essentially this: Black Muslim boys and girls stand
muster for cleanliness and decorum each morning. The
classes are separated, boys in one section, girls in the other,
and the students' day is divided between religious and secular
education. They are taught both English and Arabic; they
are drilled in the history of the black man in Africa and
America. Then they are taught the history of the Black
Muslim movement from Fard down to Minister Malcolm X.

In 1963 Sister Christine X, one of the directors of the
school, authored a new first reader which is now being
employed. The exercises in the book are something American educators would do well to study:

> My name is Nora X. My father's name is James X,
> and my mother is Frances X. We are Muslims. We have
> our own flag. Our flag is over there on the wall. The
> symbols on our flag are a star and a crescent.

Then the students are told to use the following words
in sentences: Allah, black, Muhammad, God, Temple, nation, flag, Armageddon, Elijah.

Other exercises in the book call for the student to write
short essays on Mr. Muhammad and other notables within
the movement. Then as the students progress through school
they are taught to link subject matter to the history of the
black man. For example, when the students are being taught
mathematics they are repeatedly reminded that much of
modern math is based on work done by the Egyptians; they
are not allowed to forget that English is not their native
tongue, that their language is Arabic, that the white man
robbed them of their tongue when he kidnaped their foreparents from Africa.

The thing that arrests me most about these schools is
that they are now turning out the first generation of youth
completely schooled in the Black Muslim doctrine. Unlike
Malcolm X, John Ali, and other prominent Muslims of
today who had to be "de-brainwashed" before they saw

the light, the movement now has several score teen-agers who have been grounded in their faith just as a devout Catholic child is reared in his. As of now the movement suffers greatly from a lack of trained leaders. Only a handful of capable men and women are available to the organization and the nature of their doctrine is such that trained Negroes are hardly apt to join. But a few more years will see the emergence of well-trained Black Muslims who, I am certain, will give the organization more administrative order than it now has.

Meanwhile the Black Muslims are bombarding Negroes all over the nation with their message to the "lost-found, so-called Negro in the wilderness of North America." For a number of years Mr. Muhammad had a weekly column in some of the nation's best Negro newspapers. Now the Muslims publish their own weekly, *Mr. Muhammad Speaks,* a thirty-six-page tabloid that has the largest circulation of any Negro newspaper being published. The Muslims also conduct a weekly radio program on stations in some forty cities throughout the nation. All this is augmented by the appearances of Malcolm X on radio and TV programs each week. All in all, the Black Muslims have covered the nation; their basic teachings are known and debated by Negroes everywhere.

On the whole, then, the state of the Nation of Islam is good; its population is growing, its economy is well into the black, and its foreign relations—though strained—are better than they have ever been before.

4. THE BLACK MUSLIMS AND
THE NEGRO REVOLT

The Separate State

On the day every television network carried scenes of Birmingham police dogs attacking Negro children, Malcolm X submitted to an interview. Asked what he thought of the events at Birmingham, Malcolm said: "Martin Luther King is a chump, not a champ. Any man who puts his women and children on the front lines is a chump, not a champ."

This was Malcolm's most inglorious hour. It will take him months of hard work to regain the ground he lost among non-Muslim Negroes with that single statement. Even the Negro moderates, those who disapprove of the direct-action technique, were silenced by the dogs, fire hoses, and club-swinging policemen. Since Birmingham I have been on a lecture tour that carried me to eight major cities in as many states; I found that Negroes were melted into one by the fire of that battle; I saw a unity I have never seen in rank-and-file Negroes before; I felt a mutual love that is all but unknown among Negroes; I sensed a dislike for white people that borders on the disgraceful. Martin King—and we know his strengths as well as his weaknesses—triggered Birmingham. This nation's Negroes were with him. If he was a "chump," so were we all.

Malcolm's statement had the effect of making every Negro who wept when he saw dogs attacking Negro children feel like a moral idiot; Malcolm's analysis—if proper—means that every Negro woman who shouted resentment when she saw her black sisters knocked to the ground is spiritually illiterate and intellectually stupid. Malcolm—in a contorted

way, to be sure—allowed himself to become one with Bull
Conner. Malcolm X, the brilliant student of mass psychology,
blundered badly.

The Black Muslims had a multiple choice at Birmingham: they could have joined us in the demonstrations;
they could have kept quiet; they could have denounced us.
I was there and watched the Black Muslim position take
shape. Minister James X of the Birmingham temple wanted
Malcolm to come and make a major speech during the
turmoil; Minister Jeremiah X, minister to the Atlanta temple and roving southern bishop for the movement, was
of much the same mind. Knowing the Black Muslim line
of authority as I do, I am certain that James and Jeremiah
reflected not only Malcolm's desire to come but Elijah
Muhammad's decision to let the Big X fly to Birmingham
if the proper stage were set. The matter was debated by
Negro non-Muslims who could have set just such a stage.
Some felt it would be a good thing to have Malcolm speak
in Birmingham, since the Klan held a rally there at the
peak of the crisis. Others felt the Black Muslims should
stay out of the picture. There was a standoff on the question, and silence prevailed. Non-Muslim Negroes knew Malcolm X could not speak in favor of integration. And they
prayed—both to Jehovah and Allah—that Big Red would
take advantage of that excellent opportunity to keep quiet.

Malcolm elected to speak against us. We were all pained
by his outburst, but now—after several weeks of reflection
—it is clear that Malcolm did precisely what he had to
do. For the Negro revolt had caught up with the Black
Muslims.

The Black Muslims came to power during a moral in-
terregnum, at a time when it seemed certain that this nation
would refuse to obey its own desegregation laws. But the
sudden new militancy of the Negro has forced an un-
scheduled confrontation between the Muslims and this republic: America must prove that it is not a nation of white
devils or perish. The Black Muslims, on the other hand,
must face the reality of change in the American way of
life. The Negro has always privately talked loud and bit-
terly about the American white man. The Black Muslims
brought that talk into the open, on television and radio,
and made it plain for all to see and hear. This was good

for both the Negro and the white man: it shocked and frightened white people to hear what we have been thinking and saying about them for five hundred years; the Black Muslims were a catharsis for us, purging our innards of the bile brought on by slavery and segregation. Released from consuming anger we dropped the façade of puritan legalism and went racing into the streets screaming that defiance which is endemic to the tribe of restless natives we American Negroes most certainly are. Thus the inspired Negro students who took our fight into the streets, who shouted "now or never," have challenged the Black Muslims by interposing the theology of desegregation. In *The Negro Revolt* I described that theology in these words:

The sit-ins raged throughout the spring of 1960 and convinced even more people that direct mass action was the shorter, more effective route to their goal of desegregation. But, from an internal viewpoint, more significant than the stale coffee and soggy hamburgers was the brand of Negro that was emerging. They were no longer afraid; their boldness, at times, was nothing short of alarming. And although few people knew it, a new religion, peculiar to the Negro, was being born.

This faith, given incipient articulation by Martin Luther King, was the culmination of a hundred years of folk suffering. Like all faiths, it is peculiar to the people who fashioned it; it was a hodgepodge, as every faith is, of every ethical principle absorbed by my people from other cultures. And so the best of Confucius, Moses, Jesus, Gandhi, and Thoreau was extracted, then mixed with the peculiar experience of the Negro in America. The result was a faith that justified the bus boycott and inspired Negro college students to make a moral crusade out of their right to sit down in a restaurant owned by a white man and eat a hamburger.

As Pastor Kelly Miller Smith walked to the lectern to begin his Sunday sermon, on that first Sunday of March, 1960, in Nashville, Tennessee, he knew his parishioners wanted and needed more than just another spiritual message. The congregation—most of them middle-class Americans, many of them university students and faculty members—sat before him waiting, tense;

for Nashville, like some thirty-odd other Southern college towns, was taut with racial tension in the wake of widespread student demonstrations against lunch counter discrimination in department stores.

Among the worshipers in Pastor Smith's First Baptist Church were some of the eighty-five students from Fisk and from Tennessee Agricultural and Industrial University who had been arrested and charged with conspiracy to obstruct trade and commerce because they staged protests in several of Nashville's segregated eating places. Just two days before, Nashville police had invaded Mr. Smith's church—which also served as headquarters for the demonstrators—and arrested one of their number, James Lawson, Jr., a Negro senior theological student at predominantly white Vanderbilt University, on the same charge.

"Father, forgive them," Mr. Smith began, "for they know not what they do." And for the next half-hour, the crucifixion of Christ carried this meaning as he spoke:

"The students sat at the lunch counters alone to eat, and when refused service, to wait and pray. And as they sat there on that Southern Mount of Olives, the Roman soldiers, garbed in the uniforms of Nashville policemen and wielding night sticks, came and led the praying children away. As they walked down the streets, through a red light, and toward Golgotha, the segregationist mob shouted jeers, pushed and shoved them, and spat in their faces, but the suffering students never said a mumbling word. Once the martyr mounts the Cross, wears the crown of thorns, and feels the pierce of the sword in his side there is no turning back.

"And there is no turning back for those who follow in the martyr's steps," the minister continued. "All we can do is to hold fast to what we believe, suffer what we must suffer if we would forgive them, for they know not what they do."

This new gospel of the American Negro is rooted in the theology of desegregation; its missionaries are several thousand Negro students who—like Paul, Silas, and Peter of the early Christian era—are braving great dangers and employing new techniques to spread the faith. It is not an easy faith, for it names the conservative

Negro leadership class as sinners along with the segrega-
tionists. Yet this new gospel is being preached by clergymen and laymen alike wherever Negroes gather.

Here, then—in the American Negro's mind and for his
loyalty—is being waged one of the several battles gods
have fought during the history of man. This particular encounter is between a home-grown Allah who is one with
black men the world over but who has a special yen for
the American Negro, and a transmuted Jesus who was born
in Judea, crucified on Golgotha's heights, rose from the
dead to ascend into heaven, but submitted to reincarna-
tion as a student sit-in. And so it is that Allah and Jesus
fight it out for the spiritual allegiance of the American
Negro at a lunch counter in Woolworth's.

This is indeed a long way from the mountains near
Olympia and the flats of Greece where the gods once romped
and fought for glory. But gods follow man; wherever man
is, wherever the great issues of man are being determined,
there also one will find the gods. Man and the issue are
now centered around the rise and current crisis of Western
civilization. The British historian-theologian Arnold Toynbee
suggests that the black Westerner may well determine the
fate of Atlantic civilization. The gods apparently agree, and
they have come to our shores to ply their wares. But Western
man, particularly the Negro, is demanding more of his gods
than man once did.

Once upon a time all the gods had to do was promise man
life after death, an eternal remission for the sins man committed on earth while trying to sing a hymn in a strange
land. But the gods can no longer get away with such shoddy
realism; men want to eat good food, sleep without being
awakened by nibbling rats, work at jobs commensurate with
their abilities, live where their earning power allows them,
and use all facilities paid for out of public funds.

"We don't want to eat a hot dog in this store," Jeremiah
X said to me as we watched scores of Birmingham young-
sters stage sit-ins; "we want the store and the ground on
which it sits."

This is the dilemma the Black Muslims now face: They
must eschew everything tinged by "integration," yet they
must seek acceptance among the black masses who are

risking their all—particularly in the South—for the sake of fuller involvement in the American mainstream. The Muslims' reply, of course, is the separate state, a place where all American black men will live, have their own government, readopt Arabic, reaccept Allah, and ready themselves for the hour when the "word" will be given and Armageddon will proceed.

The tragedy of this is that Black Muslim leaders, including Elijah Muhammad, have said they know such a state will never come into being. This admission by them relieves me of the need to discuss the impracticality of the proposal. Rather, I am engaged by the fact that the Black Muslims continue to urge Negroes to back the demands for such a state rather than act to better their plight in the nation as it now is.

Their promise of a separate state, like the chariot that was scheduled to swing low and take us home a century ago, is but another of the mirages that has kept the American Negro from digging water in the land that is his and under his feet. Black Muslims are forbidden to vote; thus they cannot help us overcome such men as Eastland and Talmadge. They are against all forms of integration; thus they cannot help us in the fight for better jobs, schools, and housing.

The Negro masses are beginning to indict the Black Muslims for impotence; they talk but cannot act; they criticize but cannot correct. Thus the Black Muslims are running the risk of becoming just another sect, an offbeat faith that expiates destiny by the shouting of voices, the stomping of feet, and the banging of tambourines. Their early promise of becoming a meaningful new faith has been made pallid by their lack of an activated social gospel. To put it bluntly, the Black Muslims are flirting with the same doom that overtook Christianity.

As the interview in Part Two shows, I have questioned Malcolm X in depth about this. He is adamant, his voice has the ring of finality. In substance, his position is this:

The Negro Revolt will fail because integration will not work; it will not work because the white man is wicked by nature and will not give Negroes full participation in American life. It is not that the white man refuses

to integrate, but that his wicked nature makes it impossible for him to give justice, equality, and freedom to other peoples. Even the victories that have been won are tricks, token integration offered to a few Negroes to quiet the Negro masses. When Negroes realize they have been tricked, that the white man has no intentions of integrating, trouble will break out. And this is when the Black Muslims will inherit the earth, particularly America. This nation could avoid all this by granting Negroes states of their own. But they are too wicked to do even that. So let Armageddon rip.

Even so, I pressed Malcolm:

LOMAX: Minister Malcolm, will the Black Muslims join picket lines and demonstrations for better jobs, housing, and schools?
MALCOLM X: Only The Honorable Elijah Muhammad can answer that.

The Friends and Followers of Malcolm X

It pains Malcolm X that most people consider him *the* spokesman for the Black Muslims. Malcolm prefaces all his public statements with the phrase, "The Honorable Elijah Muhammad teaches us that . . ."; he attributes his every thought and action to the teachings of Mr. Muhammad. "The Messenger is the Prophet of Allah," Malcolm once explained to me, "and I am but Elijah's servant."

Following a Los Angeles TV debate between Malcolm X, two other Negroes, and me, my aunt invited some fifty people to meet the members of the panel at her home. Malcolm X appeared and of course became the center of attraction. The guests were upper-middle-class Negroes— doctors, lawyers, teachers, professionals all. Some ten white persons were also present. One woman asked Malcolm why he prefaced his remarks by saying, "The Honorable Elijah Muhammad teaches us that . . ."

"Because," Malcolm said cuttingly, "Mr. Muhammad is

everything and I am nothing. When you hear Charlie Mc-
Carthy speak, you listen and marvel at what he says. What
you forget is that Charlie is nothing but a dummy—he is
a hunk of wood sitting on Edgar Bergen's lap. If Bergen
quits talking, McCarthy is struck dumb; if Bergen turns
loose McCarthy will fall to the floor, a plank of sawdust
fit for nothing but the fire. This is the way it is with the
Messenger and me. It is my mouth working, but the voice
is his."

Malcolm X may well be Elijah Muhammad's Charlie
McCarthy, but it was Charlie McCarthy who made Edgar
Bergen rich and famous. By the same token, observers are
convinced that whereas Elijah Muhammad is the maximum
leader of the movement, Malcolm X is the man who will
have to save the Black Muslims from becoming just another
sect or cult. Malcolm's role rests on more than his indisputa-
table ability and public presence; it is augmented by the ab-
sence of other talented men in the movement. I have met
and talked with every major figure in the Black Muslim
hierarchy, and there is not one among them who can do the
job that must be done if the organization is to make a
continuing impression on non-Muslim Negroes. This is not
to say that there are no able administrators within the
movement; on the contrary, I, for one, am convinced that
Malcolm is not a good administrator, that men like John
X are better suited than he for this role. But John X
cannot capture the mind and imagination of TV viewers
as Malcolm X has done. Both of Muhammad's sons are
extremely able, but they cannot cause the nation's press
to beat a path to Muhammad's door, as Malcolm has done.

Malcolm X now holds down three jobs: he is minister
of Temple Number Seven, New York; minister of Temple
Number Four, Washington, D.C.; and traveling bishop-
troubleshooter for the entire movement. Malcolm roams
the nation holding press conferences and being the *official
presence* wherever Muslims get into trouble with the police;
he moves between temples, making sure that internal problems are handled correctly; he moves from town to town
organizing new temples and addressing mass rallies; he has
spoken at most major universities outside the South and fills
the air waves with his beguiling jargon.

Then Malcolm commutes several times a month to Phoe-

nix, Arizona, where the asthma-stricken Elijah Muhammad now lives, for further guidance and policy conferences. Hardly a day passes that Malcolm does not speak with the Messenger from wherever he is by telephone. I know from many personal experiences that even so trivial a request as one for Malcolm to sit for an interview is cleared with The Honorable Elijah Muhammad. I also know that Muhammad sometimes says "no" and that Malcolm obeys. Many commentators make much over what they call the "New York-Chicago" cleavage within the Black Muslim movement. I am inclined to doubt the reality of that cleavage, but I am also convinced that there are stresses and strains within the movement, the same kinds of stresses and strains that afflict any organization that involves human beings.

Elijah Muhammad officially lives in Chicago but actually spends almost all of his time in Arizona. This is for reasons of health alone and talk to the contrary is untrue. From Phoenix the Messenger runs everything. Chicago is the nerve center of the movement, and Elijah activates it by telephone calls and couriers. It is now clear that Elijah has delegated to Chicago the responsibility for turning out the movement's publications and over-all policy statements. It is equally clear that the finances and other administrative chores of the movement are carried out in Chicago. Malcolm at one time carried some of these responsibilities, particularly the publishing of the Muslim newspaper, and many observers thought they saw an intraorganizational fight when these responsibilities were taken from him and given to Chicago. They are wrong; what they saw was a freeing of Malcolm X, a decision by Muhammad that Malcolm was needed as ambassador-at-large for the Black Muslims, that he should not be tied down to the responsibility of editing and publishing a weekly newspaper. This decision by Muhammad was made possible because John X, a former FBI agent and perhaps the best administrative brain in the movement, was shifted from New York to Chicago.

Raymond Sharrieff is without doubt the strong man of the movement. He is tall, big, and quiet, as a strong man should be. But his strength, too, flows down from that enigmatic man, Elijah Muhammad. Muhammad has been able to harness Malcolm X, John X, and Sharrieff to the same plow and make them pull in tandem. But once Muhammad

dies—at least so most observers feel—this triumvirate will fly apart and wreck the movement. I doubt it. The Black Muslims know the world is waiting for just this to happen, and I am positive they have already made certain that it will not happen.

The New Policy

Succession is not the major question facing the Black Muslims; the young, thinking men in the hierarchy know what the big issue is, know that they must issue a new policy statement if they are to capture the minds of the Negroes who are carrying out the current revolution. Calling the white man a devil and exhorting all Negroes to prepare for life in a separate state simply is not enough to win over the children who marched at Birmingham and all over this republic. No, if the Black Muslims are to get a hearing, they must have more than this to say.

This new policy statement is the prime concern of the Black Muslim movement. Several factors are involved:

First, the consensus among the Black Muslim hierarchy is that the current Negro demonstrations will end in bitter defeat and disappointment. These men, including Elijah Muhammad, are unalterably convinced that white America will not honor the promise of integration. Then, at least so the thinking goes, the Negro people will set off trouble; they will denounce and abandon Martin Luther King, Roy Wilkins, and James Farmer; they will turn for leadership to someone who foresaw the defeat clearly. In the meantime, however, good but misguided Negroes will take to the streets and demonstrate because they still have faith in integration, they still believe in the ability of white people to do the right thing.

I predict the Black Muslims will erect a policy of *active wait-and-see;* they will not join picket lines and participate in demonstrations, but they will take a more active part in general community life. This, I think, is the meaning behind the recent announcement that the Black Muslims are considering active participation in politics. The sug-

gestion was made during the movement's annual convention in Chicago early in the spring of 1963. It is still not clear just what the Muslims have in mind, but I see them first moving to register their people and then supporting Negro candidates who share some of the Muslims' concerns.

These candidates will not be Black Muslims; they will be "race" men who are willing to "speak out," an act that is so dear to the hearts of Muslims. These Negro candidates will not back such Muslim programs as the quest for an all-black state, but neither will they denounce the Black Muslims. Some Black Muslims may run for office, however. Malcolm X has often flirted with the idea of seeking a Congressional seat, and there are those, including me, who feel he would win if he selected the right area.

This would mean that the Black Muslims would work with political candidates who must also work with other groups, some of whom would support direct action. This would indirectly ally the Muslims with direct action and would improve their image, provided they accompanied such action with the cessation of attacks on men like Martin Luther King and Roy Wilkins. As I see it, this is the best possible position for the Black Muslims: it would ally them with the Negro push for better housing, jobs, and schools while at the same time allowing them to abstain from direct action; it would also free them to say that a separate state is still *the best* answer. Most of all, such a move would lift the Black Muslims to the level of respectability they have so long wanted. Other Negro spokesmen would have to practice summitry with the Muslims, and they would become an accepted rather than feared force in the Negro community.

A second factor involved in the Black Muslim search for a new policy turns on Akbar Muhammad, the youngest son of Elijah, who has just returned to America after two years of study at Egypt's famed Al-Azhar University. Al-Azhar is the cultural center of orthodox Islam, and its professors are the brains of that faith. It is beyond question that Elijah's position has been enhanced by Akbar's period of study there; it is just as certain that the Black Muslim movement will be affected by Akbar's return.

At this writing Akbar has been home less than a month. He is in the company of Malcolm X and will make a nation-

wide tour of Muhammad's temples, where he will lecture on traditional Islam and the influence of Africa in current world affairs.

Already his influence is being felt.

"Akbar Comes to Harlem" was the billing for a major Black Muslim rally held shortly after his return. The New York press, Negro and white, was filled with ads and special announcements inviting people to come out and hear Akbar Muhammad, the youngest son of Elijah Muhammad, report on his sojourn and studies in Africa and Egypt. Much was made of the fact that Akbar had been a student at Al-Azhar University. Even more was made of the fact that he had attended the recent summit meeting of African heads of state as a correspondent for the Muslim newspaper, *Mr. Muhammad Speaks.*

Observers of the movement were certain that his speech would be heavily pro-African, that he would argue for a closer relationship between the Black Muslim movement and traditional Islam, and that he once again would remind American Negroes of their African heritage. But Akbar Muhammad's two-hour talk before some four thousand Negroes on that Saturday afternoon in Harlem proved to be a complete surprise; further, it laid bare the only real schism there is within the Black Muslim movement.

After a highly charged introduction by Malcolm X the distinguished speaker rose. Twenty-five-year-old Akbar Muhammad is much like his father, medium brown, diminutive, slightly built. He stood at the lectern stroking his goatee during the three-minute ovation from the crowd. Then he spoke: *"As-Salaam-Alaikum."* His Arabic was exquisite. His inflection alone was enough to let the black masses know they were hearing something different from the southern-accented "Peace be with you" they hear from the ordinary Black Muslims. All up and down the block Muslims leaped into the air with ecstasy, praising Allah for the "back home" diction one of their leaders had acquired.

Akbar had been speaking a scant five minutes when the crowd became strangely silent. Elijah's son was clearly giving a new teaching, a gospel that contradicted much of what Malcolm X and others had been saying for the past few years.

"We must have unity among Negroes," Akbar said.

It is time for all of us—CORE, the NAACP, Dr. Martin Luther King, the Student Nonviolent Coordinating Committee, and the Black Muslims—to sit down together behind closed doors and unite. Negro leaders must now stop calling each other names. We must stop calling Dr. King names, and he must stop talking about us before the enemy. We may not be able to walk all the way to freedom together, but we can walk half the way together, so let's unite and walk together as far as we can.

The audience began to warm to his strange message. The notion of unity among Negro leaders—including the Muslims—was not new. Malcolm X had launched the same theme three years ago but found no takers among established Negro leaders. Recently, however, the breach had widened; Malcolm called Martin Luther King "a chump, not a champ"; King took to a New York pulpit and denounced "those among us who would have us live in a separate state." The night of that sermon King was pelted with eggs as he entered the church. Malcolm X denied that the Black Muslims were responsible for the incident but he also refused to say he was sorry that it had happened. All this was less than two weeks before the speech by Akbar.

I watched the setting as Akbar continued to speak. The stage obviously had been readied for him. This was no ordinary rally: Elijah Muhammad, Jr., had flown in from Chicago to be present, along with John X Ali, National Secretary for the movement. Ministers Jeremiah (Baltimore), Louis X (Boston), and Thomas J. (Hartford) were there. Minister Woodrow (Atlantic City) was on hand with his camera crew, and Joseph X, captain of the New York Fruit, turned his men out in full dress. This was clearly a major move, and the Muslims had worked hard to underscore its importance.

But what did it all mean?

"Now if we can unify," Akbar continued, "we can get help. I have just come from Africa," he said with a sly smile, "and I bring you a message from our African brothers. Now you newsmen get this correct. I am only bringing a message to the people, a message sent by their brothers in Africa. This is the message: Spokesmen from African

states—I'll even go so far as to tell you that they are on the west coast of Africa—told me to tell you that if you unite, they are ready to help us win our freedom. They are ready to help us with arms, men and know-how!"

The crowds at such street rallies in Harlem are always infiltrated with black nationalists, and the mere thought of Africans sending arms, men, and know-how to aid the American Negro was enough to set off rejoicing.

To the dismay of newsmen, who hoped he would go into the who, what, when, where, and how of all this, Akbar let the matter drop. Instead he turned to a discussion of the white man.

"I don't hate any man because of the color of his skin," Akbar said. "I look at a man's heart, I watch his actions, and I make my conclusions on the basis of what he does rather than how he looks."

There are two ways of interpreting what Akbar said: He could have been saying that action, not skin color, was the determining factor in any moral judgment; or he could have been spouting the Muslim line that the white man can prove he is not evil by nature by acting correctly. Either way, what Akbar was saying is a long way from the strong line preached by both Malcolm X and Elijah. And when this is coupled with Akbar's public denunciation of those Negro leaders who call other Negro leaders names, his speech takes on an even stranger character.

Akbar closed his talk with a call for unity among black men all over the world. "What we must have," he said, "is unity among American Negroes; once we get that, Africans are willing to help us with men, guns, and know-how. Then we can proceed to unity of black men all over the world."

As Akbar finished, the crowd applauded with vigor; they were all aware that they had witnessed a peculiar thing. First, Akbar had not mentioned the separate state a single time during his speech. This is indeed strange coming from the son of the Messenger, the man whose basic tenet is a call for "several states" where Negroes can form their own government. Second, Akbar did not once use the phrase, "The Honorable Elijah Muhammad." He made only one reference to his father, and that came when he said, "The Teacher tells us that we should prepare ourselves for black unity." Most of all, Akbar's talk had none of the strident

denunciations of white men that one expects to hear at a Black Muslim rally.

It was Malcolm X who pointed up the strangeness of the doctrine we had heard.

"I am guilty!" Malcolm told the crowd after Akbar finished. "I am guilty of calling other Negro leaders names. As you know, no one has done more of that recently than I have. But today we have heard a new teaching, and we are all going to abide by it. . . . Now brothers with the white buckets will pass among you. And you integrate those white buckets with some green dollar bills. Meanwhile I am going to talk to you. . . . If you help Mr. Muhammad, you are helping the man who has helped you. The Honorable Elijah Muhammad is the man who has told you the truth about yourself; The Honorable Elijah Muhammad is the man who has told you the truth about the white man . . . The Honorable Elijah Muhammad is the man who has made it possible for Brother Akbar to go to school back home in Egypt; The Honorable Elijah Muhammad is the man who tells you to stand up; The Honorable Elijah Muhammad is the man who tells you to look up; The Honorable Elijah Muhammad is the man who tells you to clean yourself up, provide for your wife and children, protect your family. The Honorable Elijah Muhammad will make you stop drinking; The Honorable Elijah Muhammad will make you stop stealing; The Honorable Elijah Muhammad will make you be true to your family; The Honorable Elijah Muhammad will get the monkey [dope addiction] off your back; The Honorable Elijah Muhammad will get this white, blue-eyed gorilla off your back!"

"Make it plain, Brother Minister, make it plain."

Black men and their women all up and down the streets shouted and jumped for joy. This was what they had come to hear in the first place. Big Red had made their cups run over. Now they were ready to go home.

The Harlem rally was Akbar's hour. Malcolm X had given the Messenger's son, the bright kid away at school in Egypt, a major New York hearing with the press in full attendance. And Akbar had acted like an Arab; he had talked traditional Islam and preached black unity. It was abundantly clear that Akbar is much more committed to Africa than he is to a separate black state here in America.

He reflects the Arabs' involvement with black unity throughout the world. And here lies the schism, for it is clear that Malcolm X is closer to Elijah Muhammad, in terms of just what the American Negro should do, than is Elijah's own son. This schism, however, is not as wide or as serious as the Muslims' detractors would have it. Elijah's big point is that the Negro should have a separate state; the Arabs simply shrug this off. But the imminent fall of white civilization is something upon which they all agree and for which they are all preparing.

One can expect, then, that the Black Muslims will become more "Islamic" and more "political" in the days just ahead. The new emphasis on traditional Islam will be primarily a matter of ritual and temple organization; the new "political" attitude will be an attempt at a social ethic that would place the Muslims in favor with the black masses without committing them to "integration" causes.

But this is a holding operation, something the Black Muslims, like God, suffer to be so. They are going to effect an accommodation with the Negro Revolt, but they are certain that the American white power structure will defraud us all. Then the Nation of Islam can say, "We told you so," and sound the bugle for Armageddon.

How sound would such a new policy be?

From an organizational point of view I think it would make sense. Not only is it the most liberal position they can possibly accommodate, but it shows that some—perhaps quite a few people—inside the movement are thinking creatively. As a non-Muslim, I have much the same reservations about the new policy as I had about the old. I don't share their total pessimism on how the Negro Revolt will end. I can foresee a situation in which the white power structure fails to yield and Negroes start trouble; that not only can happen, but it probably will happen in isolated pockets before the race issue is settled. I doubt that the trouble will be nation-wide, but even widespread rioting would not necessarily mean the triumph of the Black Muslims.

To state it bluntly, Negroes, as we have done in the past, can have a race riot without becoming Black Muslims!

Let there be no denying that such a tragedy will play into the hands of the Black Muslims; there are, indeed, grave

risks involved, and the best way to avoid them is to see to
it that the tragedy doesn't occur.

Peace Be Unto You

The Black Muslim movement is undeniably a sect, if for
no other reason than that it is dominated and run by
charismatic leadership. The Honorable Elijah Muhammad
is the mystical and powerful presence of the movement,
the meaning around which everything else occurs and orbits.
Elijah Muhammad has never claimed immortality; thus even
the Black Muslims know he will eventually die. Critics of the
movement predict that there will be a frenetic, perhaps
bloody, scramble for leadership at Muhammad's death. My
prediction is that the Black Muslim hierarchy will gather in
conclave and that they will come out with a new leader.
That leader will not be Malcolm X. Rather, I suggest that
Malcolm, John, and Sharrieff will be retained in the posts
they now occupy and a younger man—almost certainly one
of Muhammad's sons—will be the new Messenger.

There are three reasons why I feel this will prove true:

1. The mystique of the movement is that Muhammad
met and knew Allah—Fard. Thus it follows that the flesh
and blood of Muhammad has inherited the magic of that
encounter. Muhammad will be raised to sainthood, and the
Muslim gospel will continue to be prefaced with the phrase,
"The Honorable Elijah Muhammad taught us . . ." Thus
the new Messenger should be a physical reminder of Elijah.

2. John and Sharrieff are sensible, practical men. They
know the impact Malcolm has made on the American scene,
and they will keep him precisely where he is, for this is the
only way they can stay where they are.

3. Finally, I am persuaded of the morality of these Black
Muslim leaders. Think of their doctrine what one may, I
am convinced that they would no more fight publicly over
the question of leadership than would the cardinals of the
Roman Church. Indeed, I feel the conclave will move just
as the Catholic Church has often moved, that the question
of a new leader will be overshadowed by a debate over

policy. I see Malcolm, then, not as the maximum leader, but as prime minister and behind-the-scenes policy maker.

This is no cause for rejoicing. Akbar Muhammad, who I suspect will be the new Messenger, is steeped in traditional Islam. He will bring to the maximum-leadership post the zeal and determination one associates with the early Mohammedans. Followers of Allah have always been strong on internal brotherhood and notoriously short of patience and mercy toward outsiders. Those of us who have studied the movement have had to stand muster before Raymond Sharrieff, and to a man we are agreed that we would not enjoy tangling with him and The Fruit. Once Elijah is dead, I suspect the prospect of tangling with him will be even less inviting.

The events surrounding the public "silencing" of Malcolm X because of his intemperate remarks about the assassination of President Kennedy support this view. Malcolm was under strict orders not to discuss the death of the President. Malcolm defied the order and shocked the nation by saying that the slaying of Kennedy was an instance of chickens coming home to roost. For this he was silenced by The Honorable Elijah Muhammad. Actually the decision to silence Malcolm was made during a tense meeting between Elijah and his close advisers in Chicago. The order was curt, the decision final. Malcolm took the decision in stride. He still administers the affairs of the New York Temple but—as of this writing—he is religiously obeying the orders not to speak in public.

No one knows just how long the silencing of Malcolm will last. It had better not last very long if the movement is to maintain its impact. After all, Malcolm X is the only Black Muslim voice that is nationally known and generally recognized. At this writing insiders doubt that Malcolm's punishment will last more than a few weeks. One top Muslim official predicted, "Things will be back to normal shortly after New Year's."

"I'll be honest with you," Malcolm X said to me. "Everybody is talking about differences between the Messenger and me. It is absolutely impossible for us to differ. What he says is law; that is what is done. But I'll tell you this," he added. "Mr. Muhammad was with Allah, and he has been granted divine patience; he is willing to wait on God to deal with the devil. Well, the rest of us have not seen Allah; we

don't have this divine patience, and we are not so willing to wait on God. The younger Black Muslims want to see some action!"

For the first and, to my knowledge, only time Malcolm deviated from the Messenger's position when he said that. Malcolm X means it, he is not alone: Akbar means it, John X means it, Sharrieff means it, and Wallace, another son of Elijah's, means it. These men are waiting for integration to fail. This republic would do well to take them seriously.

The Black Muslims will endure but they will not prevail. Rather, they will linger for years to come and be a constant reminder of what this republic did to thousands who sought its promise. They will integrate this nation's body politic and make us continually aware of what can happen if white men don't learn to love before black men learn to hate. And maybe one day before I die we can all join together —black and white and Malcolm X—and say, *"As-Salaam-Alaikum."* That is to say, peace be unto you.

PART TWO

THE PROPHET'S VOICE

1. MUHAMMAD
AT ATLANTA

"Come and see and hear the most fearless black man in America today; the man who is going to defy the Ku Klux Klan!"

This is the way the Black Muslims billboarded Elijah Muhammad's now-famous "Atlanta Speech" of 1961. For when it was announced that Muhammad was to speak in Atlanta, the Klan issued a statement that they, too, would hold a rally and a march on the same day, at the same time. The Black Muslims' propaganda machinery went into action, and the Atlanta Speech was advertised as a major confrontation between Elijah and the Klan. Something a little different from that is what actually occurred.

Malcolm X flew into Atlanta several days before the scheduled meeting and began talks with police and other city officials. Malcolm was assured that the police would enforce law and order, that the Black Muslims could proceed with their meeting without fear of trouble from the Klan or anyone else.

Even so, the Black Muslims took advantage of every opportunity to dramatize their presence and activities. Long before the meeting began members of The Fruit of Islam took up posts on rooftops overlooking the route Muhammad would travel to Magnolia Hall. Even more Fruit cordoned the hall itself. With a seating capacity of only five hundred, the auditorium was jammed hours before the meeting began; another two thousand people lined up along the dirt road leading to the auditorium and heard the speech over loud-speakers. They would have fared just as well had they stayed home since the entire five-hour speech was broadcast over a local Negro-oriented radio station.

95

*The expectation mounted as word came that Muhammad
had landed at the airport; several minutes later it was announced that Muhammad was taking a few moments of ease
at the home of the local minister; then word came that The
Honorable Elijah Muhammad was en route to the temple.*

*The Fruit of Islam formed themselves into a double column
that stretched from the platform inside the auditorium, out
the front door, down the steps, and across the sidewalk to
the curb where Elijah would disembark.*

*As the crowd cheered, a long black limousine pulled up
to the auditorium and Elijah Muhammad—a five-foot-five,
unimpressive little man—along with a retinue of some six
members of his family swept into the building down the
corridor formed by The Fruit. The applause inside the
temple was loud and sustained; nervously adjusting his bow
tie, Elijah Muhammad, the Messenger of Allah, took several
bows before the people resumed their seats.*

*After a long and impassioned introduction by Malcolm
X, Elijah Muhammad rose to speak. Most of that long,
rambling lecture follows. It is a full statement of Black
Muslim doctrine replete with attacks on Negro leaders—
Negro preachers in particular. Herein we will find a detailed account of how the evil black scientist Yakub created
the white world; we learn why the white race has endured
for so long; but most of all Elijah used the Atlanta Speech
to make an impassioned plea to Negroes to become "fearless." [Observers feel that Muhammad's repetitious urging
that Negroes cease to fear white people is one of his strongest
attractions for the Negro masses.]*

*Of particular interest, at least to me, is the Paulinean
stance Elijah Muhammad assumes in this speech. He begins
by offering greetings of peace and the good life; then he goes
on to thank his local minister, Jeremiah X, for having arranged
this meeting. This done, Muhammad links the Black Muslims
with the "725 million more brothers and sisters in the
World of Islam," and issues a special note of thanks to those
of his followers who have come from as far away as California.*

*Finally, I wish to underscore the closing of this speech:
"I am God's last Messenger to you." "You must accept Allah
as God." This is the only time I have encountered the
doctrine of Elijah as the last Messenger. But it bolsters my*

Malcolm X addressing a Harlem rally protesting crime. Many civic and elected officials share the platform with him, look on as Malcolm X says, "Dope, prostitution, and numbers could not flourish here in Harlem without the knowledge of the police!"

Malcolm X raising money during a Washington, D. C., rally at which Elijah Muhammad spoke. Black Muslims give a portion of their wages to the temple each week, and these donations are the movement's major source of income. However, Muslims do raise additional funds at rallies and bazaars.

A Muslim meeting at Urlene Arena, Washington, D. C. Malcolm X confers with Wallace Muhammad.

Muslim women at Urlene Arena meeting.

(Photo by Robert L. Haggins)

Malcolm X speaking at Harvard Law School. All over the nation he has told such audiences of the Black Muslims' teaching.

(Photo by Robert L. Haggins)

Black Muslims demonstrating in front of courthouse during trial of one of their brothers.

Members of The Fruit of Islam stand inspection.

Malcolm X "makes it plain" at Temple Number Seven in Harlem.

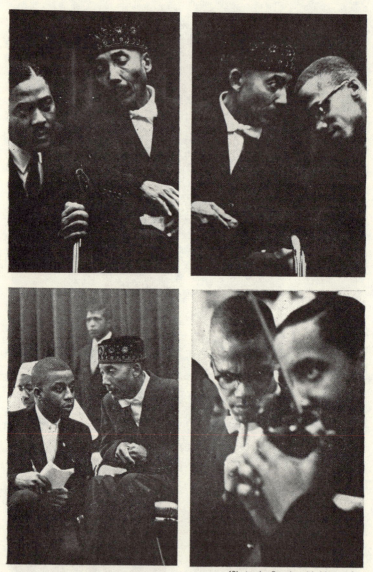

(Photos by Eve Arnold, Magnum)

Elijah Muhammad, who makes all major decisions, confers with his chief aides: *(top left)* Raymond Sharrieff, chief of The Fruit of Islam; *(top right)* Malcolm X; *(bottom left)* National Secretary John X; *(bottom right)* Elijah Muhammad, Jr., gives orders to The Fruit of Islam by walkie-talkie, while Malcolm X listens.

(Photo by Eve Arnold, Magnum)

Malcolm X makes phone call from Muslim store in Chicago.

(Photo by Eve Arnold, Magnum)

Minister Henry X takes Muslim youths on tour of the Museum of Natural History. "This was our culture before the white man kidnaped us," he tells them.

(Photo by Eve Arnold, Magnum)

Four Muslim sisters have dinner at a temple restaurant.

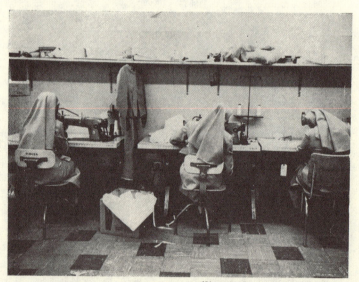

(Photo by Eve Arnold, Magnum)

Muslim women making their own costumes—long flowing dresses and headpieces.

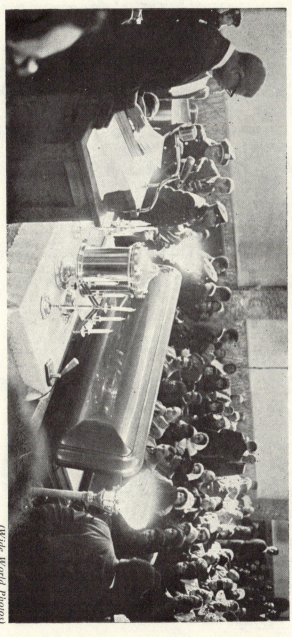

Actor Ossie Davis delivers a eulogy for Malcolm X during funeral services for the Black Nationalist leader, who was slain on February 21, 1965.

suggestion that when he dies, Muhammad will still be "The Messenger" and that the new leader of the movement will be a younger man, a titular head, while strong men like Malcolm X and Raymond Sharrieff carry the load.

As-salaam-alaikum: In the name of Allah, the most Merciful God, to whom all holy praises are due, the Lord of all the worlds; the most Merciful Finder (of) and Lifegiver to the Lost-found, mentally dead so-called Negroes here in the Wilderness of North America.

My Beloved Brothers and Sisters:

I am more than honored by your presence here this afternoon and your sincere welcome to me and to my followers here in this great city of Atlanta.

I thank Allah for Minister Jeremiah, my faithful minister here whose tireless efforts in Atlanta and throughout the South have made this great gathering here today possible. The work that Minister Jeremiah has been doing here in the South has pleased Allah, and it has pleased me too.

Year after year I receive letters from many converts here in Atlanta, and I know that the Word of Allah is spreading rapidly among our people here in the South because of the ever increasing volume of your letters to me.

And, my beloved people, I want you to know that those of you here in Atlanta and in other parts of the South who accept Islam, which is the true religion of Almighty God, are not alone. Not only do you have a fast-growing number of brothers and sisters in all of the Northern cities, but you have 725 million more brothers and sisters in the World of Islam.

I am also thankful to my followers who have traveled here to Atlanta to be with me today from my various temples throughout America, and especially the caravan of young Muslims who motored over 2,000 miles all the way from Los Angeles, California, to be here on this grand occasion.

My followers are with me wherever I go, and it is wonderful to have such sincere people who will follow you all around the country like this because it shows unity, and it also shows there is no religion that can produce unity like the unity produced by Islam. Yes, today the Muslims

are in all the major cities of America, and if you look around in the smaller cities you will find us there also. Just walk around saying, "As-Salaam-Alaikum," and pretty soon someone will reply, "Wa-Alaikum-Salaam."

Beloved brothers and sisters, again I must thank Allah for permitting me to be in your presence here in Atlanta this afternoon. I am thankful also to the Atlanta Police Department for the courtesies they have shown us here in this city, and I want everyone to know we are a people who are grateful to anyone who is nice to us, and peaceful toward us. We are a people of peace. We are seeking to spread brotherly love among the so-called Negroes for it is they who have been deprived of brotherly love. We (Muslims) have come through the same trials and tribulations as they have, and now we want them to see and share the brotherhood that Islam has given us.

Islam is not a new religion. Islam is not a religion that has been organized by the white man. Islam is the religion of God Himself, and Islam is the religion of all the prophets of God, from Adam to Muhammad (the last). Islam was the religion of Moses, Noah, Abraham, and Jesus. Islam will be the last of the three great religions (Buddhism, Christianity, and Islam) that now dominate the earth.

Islam must be the last of these three great religions because God Himself is the Author of Islam, and Islam is to bring peace and contentment after this war and trouble-making world which you now know has been destroyed . . . and you can see that this trouble-making world is already on its way out.

Islam has not made great progress for the past 6,000 years because this is the religion that God Himself would spread in the "last days." If Islam had been forced upon all the people of the earth during the past 6,000 years there would not have been any "World of Christianity," there would not have been any "World of Buddhism" . . . and there would never have been anything like the "Caucasian World." Islam would have prevented their progress. God Himself has held Islam "in check" to give these other "worlds" free reign during the past 6,000 years.

But, Islam was the religion of the black people who lived before Adam was made, as far back as 66 trillion years ago when the earth and the moon were together and formed one

and the same planet . . . and which at that time was called "moon" instead of earth.

According to the word of Allah to me, one of our wise black scientists was upset over the dialect the people were speaking, and he wanted to change the language and make all of the people speak the same dialect. He became angry because he could not get the others to go along with him, and when he saw that he could not accomplish what he wanted, he drilled a huge shaft into this planet for about four or five thousand miles deep, and filling that hole with high explosives he set it off, with the intention of destroying all civilization. He thought he would get rid of us.

That part of the planet which we call "moon" today was blasted 12,000 miles from its original pocket that it had been rotating in at the time of the explosion, and this part that we call "earth" today dropped 36,000 miles from that pocket and found another pocket and started rotating again . . . (it all happened in the twinkling of an eye) . . . and that part (moon) that was blasted away dropped all of its water upon this part (earth), and this is why three-fourths of the earth's surface today is covered by water, and also why there is no life on the moon.

We are the people who devised that great destruction of our planet. That part (moon) that you see up there in the sky shining at night was once joined with this part (earth) that we now live on. Before the explosion the entire planet was then called "moon." (Not really by the word "moon" that we use today, but by a word in Arabic that means practically the same thing.) We will have another great destruction, and we will provide that one too. We ourselves (the black nation) are a people who can never be destroyed. There never was a time when we (the black nation) didn't exist. We don't have any birth record of the black nation. We have no beginning and we have no ending. So don't talk about getting rid of the Black Man, because you cannot do it.

Again I say, we are happy to be in Atlanta today, the capital of Georgia . . . my birth state. I was born in this state, and grew up in this state. I was a grown man, married and the father of children even before I left this state. So don't try and make me acquainted with Georgia. I am already acquainted with Georgia.

This great city of Atlanta with its five colleges, institu-

tions of learning, is one of America's most important cities, and is even the gateway to the South. We thank the city for permitting us to enter it, and the courtesy of the police department, and the mayor of this great city, and the governor of the state. We are happy to be called one of your own state-borned sons.

My beloved people, I am one of your brothers; I am not a foreigner, but I have a Divine Message from the Lord of the Worlds that sounds foreign to you because you have not heard it before.

I want you to know that we so-called Negroes are the people who have been on this planet for trillions of years. I say so-called Negro because you are not a Negro. You are members of the Asiatic Nation, from the Tribe of Shabazz. There is no such thing as a race of Negroes. This is a false name given you during slavery by your slave master, who, after robbing you completely of your knowledge of your homeland, your parents, and your culture, called you "Negro" or Nigger because that word means something that is "NEUTER" or "NEUTRAL." Therefore you are now a little group of people on this earth who stand out because you have become neutralized by ignorance of yourself and your own kind, and of your enemy. You are "neutral" . . . not united with yourselves, among yourselves, nor are you united with your own people of your own world.

Since ignorance of self and hatred of self makes you reluctant to unite with your own kind, and despite your love and worship of your slave master he will not let you unite with him . . . thus you are in the middle, standing alone, neutralized by your own lack of knowledge, unacceptable to either friend or foe . . . NEGROES!!!

This is why you are called NEGRO. The slave master gave you this name because he understood the meaning of it, although Webster has cunningly kept you away from the true meaning of it by saying it refers to black people . . . and especially the black African who has no education or independence.

My dear brothers and sisters, and distinguished educators of Atlanta, you have often wondered why you had to call yourselves by this name "Negro." It has been due to the fact that you didn't know its origin and you didn't know your origin. You have been asleep. You don't know

whom you are from, where you are from, where you are going, how you should stand, how you should sit . . . you know nothing at all but what your slave master chooses to tell you, and since he tells you only that which will benefit himself and his own kind, you have been made into a NEUTRAL person . . . a shiftless, helpless NEGRO.

If the white man says to you, "Johnny, go back home, I have no work for you today," you go back home and sit down and wait for the white man to send for you (when he sees fit) to come back and work on his job. You don't try to create a job for yourself. You are shiftless because the lack of "proper" education and self-knowledge has left you lifeless (mentally, economically, and otherwise).

I am not making fun of you. I am trying to lead you to the point where you can see the basic cause of your condition. I am one of you. I came through the same trials and tribulation and the same hell that you did. What I say about you I am also saying it about myself. I am your brother; I am here, if necessary, to give my life to save yours. I am not running from death. I am running to save your life. So take me for a friend and not an enemy.

You must learn to make jobs for yourselves so that the next time "boss" tells you he does not have any work for you, you can tell him that you are going to do some work for yourself.

Three hundred years under the persecution of your slave master has made you into a blind, deaf, and dumb . . . and an absolutely "dead" people. He has taught you to eat the rotten and worse type of foods, even the flesh of that poisonous animal, the swine (pork) . . . filling your stomach with this poison meat (pork) has deteriorated you physically, mentally as well as morally. The Arab word for the pig is "Khainsuer." ("Khain" means "I see," and "suer" means "very foul.") This word thus means "I see something that is very foul, filthy, diseased" . . . something that is not fit to be eaten by intelligent, civilized people.

Your slave master reared you on this poisonous meat, which has dulled your brains, and you ceased to think about your past history, and then you were deprived easily of the knowledge of your own God and your own religion. Thus it became easy for the slave master to deprive you also of the knowledge of your own kind, and the knowledge

of his kind. Now you don't know the way back to your own kind, and his kind won't accept you . . . so they call you Nigger or Negro, which means deaf, dumb, and blind . . . neutral, dead, lifeless.

We, the Nation of Islam, who believe in freedom, justice and equality stand not only before you today, but before the entire world as we declare this truth about the American so-called Negroes. The nations of earth are faced today with a worse problem than has ever presented itself in the history of mankind, and the primary ingredient of this great "world problem" involves the condition and position of the so-called Negro here in America . . . 20 million ex-slaves who have become a nation within a nation and who are now crying out for something that they can call their own. This is creating a problem not only for America, but for the entire world, and that problem is: how to give you a knowledge and understanding of yourself, teach you the knowledge of your own God and your own religion, and to teach you the knowledge of your own nation so that you can make a stand for yourselves as other nations are making for themselves.

This problem is so delicate and complicated that only God Himself can solve it. I am not a man who has grabbed a suitcase with a bible in it upon my own impulses. No! I stand before you as a man who has been chosen for you by God Himself. I did not choose myself. This must be made clear! The Divine Revelation which I have received and which I am preaching to you and to the entire world came to me from the Mouth of God.

I did not see Him in a vision and receive my mission in a vision as others before me received theirs. I was in the Presence of God for over three years, and I received what I am teaching you directly from His Mouth.

Let the infidels curse and swear at me. Let the infidels go on the warpath of propaganda against Elijah, but I warn you: "You better listen today to him who has received his instructions directly from the Mouth of Almighty God." I did not receive this gospel from a paper, nor a book, nor from a vision, nor from an angel, but directly from the Mouth of Almighty God Himself.

My beloved people: I know your problems and your burdens; I know your problems and your burdens; I know what you go through; you don't have to tell me . . . for I

have the ABSOLUTE CURE for all your problems and ailments. All you have to do is listen to what I say, and then
jump up on your feet and follow me.

I don't want you to be too proud, as others were in
former times; they were too proud to follow the words of
the prophets. I don't want you to be like that. I want you
to place more value on your life than they did. Think something of your future, and your children, and your people.
Accept Allah and His religion and follow me and I will lead
you to Him and to a heaven right here on this earth. Come
and follow me, and you will not have to wait until after you
die to see God, nor will you have to wait until after you die to
enjoy a heaven somewhere up in the sky.

Beloved brothers and sisters: after receiving this Divine
Revelation that I am teaching you from the Mouth of God,
I have not stopped one day for the last twenty-nine years.
I have been standing, preaching to you throughout these
past twenty-nine years, while I was free and even while I
was in bondage. I spent three and one-half years in the
federal penitentiary and also over a year in the city jail
for teaching this truth. I was also deprived of a father's
love for his family for seven long years while I was running
from hypocrites and other enemies of this word and revelation of God, and which will give life to you and put you on
the same level with all other civilized and independent
nations of this earth . . . and this is the greatest desire of
Almighty God Allah and Elijah Muhammad. This afternoon
I want to teach the so-called American Negroes the true
knowledge of themselves that will lift them from the bottom
and place them back at the top of civilization.

I know how you feel. I know how you think. You think
as Ezekiel says of you. Ezekiel says, "This whole House of
Israel, they say their hope was lost and they were cut off
from their fathers." You are a people who are all hopeless
because you think there is no hope for you. You think that
because you have been cut off from your own people for
so long there is no chance of you ever uniting or of ever
becoming anything but what you now are. I say you are
wrong. The God of your Fathers, whose proper name is
Allah, will strengthen you and cause you to stand upon
your own feet as an independent people in the eyes of other
people on this earth.

This Truth that I am teaching will raise you up from the grave, not out of the earthly grave, but out of the "grave of ignorance." You just need the knowledge of yourself, your own God and your own religion. God has missioned me to give you this Truth: freedom, justice, and equality.

These are the things I must teach you about: freedom first, because you have never been free here in America. You know nothing about the pleasures or happiness of a free person. You know nothing about justice. You know nothing about equality, or being equal with other civilized nations of earth.

I know you and your thoughts about me and what I teach. Inwardly, some of you are with me 100 per cent, but outwardly you are not. Why? Because you have the greatest enemy over you a man can have, and that is "FEAR." Fear is your greatest enemy. You were filled with fear of your slave master when you were little babies, over 400 years ago when our fathers were brought in chains to the Western Hemisphere on a slave ship that was named "The Good Ship Jesus." The captain of that ship was an English Christian named John Hawkins.

The American white people had come to this country from Europe and had already begun to subdue the Indians. We were brought here to a people who could not speak our language nor could we speak theirs. Thus the language of our forefathers was soon destroyed, and you know nothing about it today. The language of the slave master was forced upon our foreparents, and they were brought up also wearing the names of the slave masters. Today, you are still speaking their language and wearing their names.

During 300 long years of slavery you were deprived of the privilege of even going to church, and there were no such things as schools for you in those days. Besides depriving you of education the slave master did not teach you about God, Jesus, and the Holy Ghost that he is now teaching you about today. You were never allowed to sit with them in their churches until just a few years ago.

Beloved brothers and sisters, think over this: for over 400 years you had no knowledge of yourselves, no knowledge of your own religion, and no knowledge of the biblical prophecies and predictions pertaining to the "lost people" who would be on this planet until the last days, and whom

God Himself would have to search for and then save them from the clutches of their enemies. You have never been given a knowledge of that because your slave master knew those prophecies were speaking about you (the American so-called Negroes).

For less than 100 years now a little bit of the Christian religion has been taught to you in a diluted form, but never the full text of it. You have never learned the prophetic fate of Christianity, nor do you know anything about the Caucasian people who have translated the bible into their language. Yet, you are a people who think you know all about the bible, and all about Christianity, and you are even foolish enough to believe that nothing is right but Christianity.

Your slave master tampered with the words of the bible; he "translated" it; he "revised" it; he fixed the reading of it to make you a worse slave than your foreparents were. The slave master is the "god" who "sent" some of your fellow slaves to preach to you. Their favorite text was, "Servant, obey your master." But he didn't really have to preach that because the lashes of the whip upon the backs of your parents for 300 years had beaten them into obedient submission.

But, my beloved brothers and sisters, the Christian religion you now are believing in so strongly came down to you from your slave masters. They kept that religion and its secrets guarded from your parents' ears for 300 years. What was then so sacred in Christianity? What was so sacred in the bible which they kept locked away from the slaves? What was so sacred about these things that the slave master did not want his slaves to read or even hear preached? If it was so good, why didn't he want his slave to hear this good then? Why didn't he want his slave to believe in God then?

First of all, the slave master did not want the slaves to know the truth about God nor about His true religion, fearing that the slave would then begin looking for his God to deliver him from his white oppressors.

I know some of you are afraid to listen to this truth but I am going to preach it to you until you are free of that fear. A man told me a few years ago that I would be wasting my time to come to Georgia. He said that the Negroes in Georgia were more afraid of white people than you will find any-

where else on this earth. I told him that I myself was born in
Georgia and did not see why they should be afraid of the
white man. I told him that I was a grown man, married and
with two children when I left Georgia. I also told him that
they need not fear the white man; the only thing they need
to fear is the fear within themselves.

I say to you that your fear of the white man is THE
GREAT EVIL. Fear is of such nature that it will make you
deprive yourself of your own salvation. Fear is the enemy
that will make you stoop and bring yourself to disgrace
before the world. Fear is the real enemy that you and I
should throw into the garbage can.

My beloved brothers and sisters, how could you accept
of God, Jesus and the Holy Ghost. How do you know? I
am not asking you to answer these questions, because God
has missioned me to answer them for you. You don't know
the answers. All you know is what you have heard your slave
master say.

You say Christianity is the right religion and that you
believe in God the Father, God the Son, and God the Holy
Ghost. You believe that this Jesus is God's son, and that
He gave His son to save you. You say that the Holy Ghost
"overpowered" a virgin girl named Mary, yet you don't
call the child the son of the Holy Ghost, you call the child
"the son of God." You charge God with being the father
of this virgin girl's child.

My beloved brothers and sisters, how could you accept
a religion that teaches you to believe the God of Righteousness was responsible for making a virgin girl in Palestine
pregnant with a child 2,000 years ago, called this child his
"son," and let this "son" die for the sins of the wicked
world?

When a man is not married to a woman and he com-
mits such a sinful act it is called adultery. God is not married
to a woman, and if He commits such a sinful act that
produces a child out of wedlock, which actually opens the
gateway of adultery to the entire world, then it is a shame to
ask me to believe in that god.

We in Islam do not ascribe "sonship" to Almighty God,
because He has no son. All of us are His "spiritual" children, but He has no physical son. To say that God has
produced a physical son out of wedlock (without being

married to the mother of that son), and then placed this son before our eyes and said, "This is my beloved son; all who believe in him and follow him shall be saved," actually opens the gateway for all kinds of adultery and other indecent acts.

God had already told His prophet Moses that the people should be stoned to death for adultery. Now if God had come 2,000 years after giving the law against adultery to Moses, and after "courting" or "overpowering" Mary, and she was a virgin girl who had never been touched by any man, and yet she became pregnant with His child, and that child is the flesh and blood "son" of God . . . then the Christians are charging God Himself with having committed adultery with Mary.

This just could not have been done if God was a spirit. If He was a spirit He could not father a flesh and blood son. He would have to have a son like Himself. If He was a spirit, then His son would have to be a spirit too. And, if He did beget a son by Mary, then all other women would be justified in producing sons that same way, by committing adultery and then blaming it on the "spirit."

The Western World is always defending Christianity and they mock me and other Islamic teachers. They do not want Islam preached to you, but the reason you are hearing it today is because it is time. This preaching of Islam to you today cannot be stopped; it is like the rising of the sun . . . right on time.

Here in America there are also three and one-half million indirect believers in Islam, in the secret order called Shriners, or Higher Masons. When you take the thirty-third degree in masonry you are no longer called a Mason; you are then called a Moslem Son, and in that order (or degree) you are taught the prayers of the Moslems and you come under the teachings of Islam. In that High Degree you are taught to turn your face Eastward, toward the Holy City of Mecca in Arabia. All of this is part of the Moslem religion, Islam.

Today, Islam must be taught to the so-called American Negroes. You must learn about this religion, because there can be no judgment of the devil and his wicked world until after you (the lost people of God) have heard the truth about God and the truth about the devil as I am teaching you today. It is only after you have heard the teachings of

Islam that you can make a wise choice between God and the devil.

We are not trying to force you to accept Islam, but we are trying to make you realize that we know what is in store for the world; we know what tomorrow will bring. Therefore, we are not in fear of losing our lives, but we will lay down our lives this very minute for the truth. We are not running from death; we are running only to save lives . . . YOUR LIVES!!!

You must have freedom, justice, and equality. You cannot be free as long as you are calling yourselves by your slave master's name; you cannot be free as long as you do not know who you are; you cannot be free as long as you do not know your own people; you cannot be free as long as you don't know how to even ask for freedom.

Beloved brothers and sisters, God has given me the key that will open the door of freedom, justice, and equality that has been locked against you. You must be taught a knowledge of your own God. My mission is to make you acquainted with Him, to prepare you to meet Him face to face.

God is not a mystery today; He is not something invisible. He is not a spirit. He is not something other than flesh and blood; He is in the flesh and in the blood. God is a human being! God would have no joy or pleasure in humans (us) if He Himself were something other than a human being. God would have no joy or pleasure in the material universe if He Himself were other than material.

The devil is also a flesh and blood human being. The devil is not an invisible spirit. The bible and the Holy Quran both plainly state that God is going to destroy the devil in a Lake of Fire in "the last days." If the devil was an invisible spirit he could not be destroyed. You can destroy a man but you cannot destroy a spirit. So I repeat to you, my beloved brothers and sisters, God and the devil both are flesh and blood human beings.

There is no such thing as seeing God or the devil after you die. There is no such thing as a heaven up in the sky or a hell down in the ground. All of that is fantasy, false stories made up by your slave master to further enslave you. God is a man! The devil is a man! Heaven and hell are two conditions, and both are experienced in this life

right here on this earth. You have already suffered the worse kind of hell in the hands of the only real devil!

It is the devil who did not want you to know this truth that God has missioned me to teach my people. He is afraid that when you learn his real identity you will then separate yourselves from him and thereby escape the fiery destruction God has prepared for him. He wants to keep you from your salvation in the hereafter. He knows that without this truth that I am teaching you, you could never avoid the fire that God has ordained for him and enter into the Hereafter. And by HEREAFTER, we mean the Kingdom of Righteousness that God will establish "here" on this earth "after" the devil has been destroyed in the Divine Lake of Fire.

Beloved brothers and sisters, it has been predicted by all the prophets that God is coming. Well, if God is coming (and He must be coming because the whole world claims to be *"looking"* for Him), then He must be something visible. If He is an invisible spirit then the world wouldn't be *"looking"* for Him to come. The world couldn't say, "We will *see* Him" . . . because we don't *"look"* for a spirit, we *feel* for a spirit.

If God is a spirit and He says He made Adam in His own image and likeness, then I say to you Adam would have been a spirit. But God did not make a spirit; He made a man like Himself. Man looks like God and God looks like man because God is a man.

Man acts like God; he acts with power. Man does not just sit down and wait for the wheat to grow itself, harvest itself, make itself into flour, bake itself, and then bring itself to him to eat, does he? No!!!

Man plants the wheat, man cultivates it, man threshes it, man grinds it into flour, man bakes the bread, and then man eats it. If man sits all day in the house waiting for a spirit to produce that bread he would starve to death. No spirit in heaven or in hell will bring you bread . . . and no spirit in heaven or in hell will bring you freedom, justice, or equality.

I say to you, my beloved brothers and sisters, your slave master and his imps (the Negro preachers) have blinded you by such ignorant teachings and today you are still foolishly sending your praises and your prayers to an invisible God who is supposed to be somewhere out in space,

and who cannot be found by you until after you die. And, this same ignorant doctrine has you believing there is an invisible devil down in the earth somewhere beneath your feet . . . while in reality the devil is right here on top of the earth, walking around on two feet like you are, and you are looking at him every day.

God is a man, a flesh and blood being, but He is a Divine Being. Why do we call God a Divine Being? Because He is a being like we are but His wisdom, power, and other capabilities and attributes are Supreme . . . making Him the Highest Power, the Supreme in Power, or Supreme Power. He is a being like ourselves, but He has the Divine Capacity of exercising His Power or to project through His Power the powers of the Universe . . . and therefore we call Him the Supreme Being and the God of the Universe. He has the Divine Power to will whatever He wishes and to bring it into existence with His Divine Will. But He is not an invisible spirit somewhere up in the sky. His home is right here on this earth.

I would defy any spirit outside the spirit that is in a man to do anything for me or to me. I would defy any devil that is outside of a man to do anything for me or to me. But I do recognize the devil in these that can do us harm and have done us harm. No spirit independent of man can do us harm or good.

Beloved brothers and sisters, let us bring our minds out of the sky; let us stop being spooky; let us learn to face reality; let us look around here on this earth as other intelligent and civilized people are doing. Here in Atlanta is the seat of education for the so-called Negroes in this country. Yet most Negroes here are still locked into the most crowded and undesirable areas. Therefore, I would like to know what are our educated people doing with this education to elevate the living standards of your own people, and to eliminate the misery and poverty yet suffered by the so-called Negro masses who do not have education?

You who are college graduates, and you who are educators and instructors here in Atlanta, Georgia: I would like for you to tell me what you are doing with this education you have received from the white man toward making your own people more independent? What are you doing for your people with your education? Should not you take

that education to unite your people and bring them up out of the "mud of ignorance," and make them an independent people? But with all your education you yourself are still dependent upon your slave master for a job, and for your food, clothing and shelter. With your education, you have enough land and farmers to do something about the condition of the so-called American Negro.

But you must first agree that the most important ingredient has been omitted from your education, and that is the knowledge of God, the devil, of yourself, and of your enemy. Accept Allah and His true religion (Islam), and come and follow me. I am God's Messenger to you. I have the keys to your salvation. Come and follow me and I will show you how to use your education, your skills and talents, for the good of your own people and yourself.

In the unity and harmony and Brotherhood created by the religion of Islam, it is easy for us to pool our knowledge and finance to set up farms and grow food to feed our people; we can set up factories to manufacture our own necessities, and other businesses with which we can establish trade and commerce and become independent as other civilized people are. Then, in this way you will be using your education to bring your people out of the slums and the breadlines. They will cease to be the "last hired and the first fired," when you use your education to make jobs for them.

I thank you, my beloved brothers and sisters, for being here this afternoon, and listening so attentively to this truth. I am God's last Messenger to you. You must accept Allah as God. You must know that Islam is your religion. Come and follow me; let me teach you, and I will put 20 million so-called American Negroes overnight on the road to success . . . on the road toward complete independence in a home of your own, where you will never any more have to beg anyone for freedom, justice, or equality.

Thank you, my beloved brothers and sisters. May Allah forever bless you, as I leave you with the greetings of the peaceful and the righteous: As-Salaam-Alaikum . . . which means, "Peace be unto you."

2. MALCOLM X
AT HARVARD

This 1960 speech, delivered by Malcolm X before a jam-packed Harvard Law School Forum, comes from what I have called the Black Muslims' "rasping" period. These were their early days on the national scene, and it would be interesting to find out if Malcolm would make just such a speech now.

Malcolm is clearly on the defensive in the first half of his long talk; he is responding to criticism rather than spreading his own gospel. It is only after he has answered charges that the Black Muslims are not orthodox Muslims; only after he has denied that the Black Muslims teach hate; and after he has put the Negro middle class in their place for their criticism of him—only after all this does Malcolm get down to what he really went to Harvard to say.

In essence it is this: The American Negro must have a separate state. This is the only way white men can atone for their sins and escape destruction; this is the only way Negroes can return to their own.

The Harvard Speech is the best statement—and defense —of the proposed all-Negro state that the Black Muslims have issued. It shows why I suggest that the Black Muslims are completely "Americanized" in their aims and approaches. Indeed, the reader will get a good chuckle when Malcolm delivers a blistering attack on non-American Moslems, some one hundred thousand of them he says, who have migrated to this country but have been unable to gather converts. Then Malcolm reminds them that Elijah has been able to garner thousands. So then, Malcolm continues, does this not mean that The Honorable Elijah Muhammad is indeed the Messenger?

MR. CHAIRMAN, LADIES AND GENTLEMEN:

We thank you for inviting us here to the Harvard Law School Forum this evening to present our views on this timely topic: THE AMERICAN NEGRO; PROBLEMS AND SOLUTIONS. But to understand our views, the views of the Black Muslims, you must first realize that we are a religious group, and you must also know something about our religion, the religion of ISLAM.

The Creator of the Universe, whom many of you call God or Jehovah, is known to the Muslims by the name ALLAH. Since the Muslims believe there is but ONE GOD, and that all the prophets came from this ONE GOD, we believe also that all prophets taught the same religion, and that they themselves called that religion ISLAM, an Arabic word that means the complete submission and obedience to the will of ALLAH.

One who practices this Divine Obedience is called a MUSLIM (commonly known, spelled, and referred to here in the West as Moslem).

There are over 725 million Muslims on this earth, predominantly in Africa and Asia, the non-white world . . . and we here in America who are under the Divine Leadership of The Honorable Elijah Muhammad, are an integral part of the vast World of Islam that stretches from the China Seas to the sunny shores of West Africa.

A unique situation faces the 20 million ex-slaves here in America because of our unique condition, thus our acceptance of Islam, and into Islam, affects us uniquely . . . differently than all other Muslim "converts" anywhere else on this earth.

Mr. Elijah Muhammad is our Divine Leader and Teacher here in America. Mr. Muhammad believes in and obeys God 100 per cent, and is teaching and working among our people to fulfill God's Divine Purpose today.

I am here at this Harvard Law School Forum this evening to represent Mr. Elijah Muhammad, the spiritual head of the fastest-growing group of Black Muslims in the Western Hemisphere.

We who follow Mr. Muhammad know that he has been divinely taught and sent to us by God Himself. We believe that the miserable plight of the 20 million black people in America is the fulfillment of divine prophecy. We be-

lieve that the serious race problem that our presence here poses for America is also the fulfillment of divine prophecy. We also believe that the presence today in America of The Honorable Elijah Muhammad, his teachings among the 20 million so-called Negroes, and his naked warning to America concerning her treatment of these 20 million ex-slaves is all the fulfillment of divine prophecy.

Therefore, when Mr. Muhammad declares that the only solution to America's serious race problem is complete SEPARATION of the two races, he is fulfilling that which was predicted by all of the biblical prophets to take place in this day.

But, because Mr. Muhammad takes this uncompromising stand, those of you who don't understand biblical prophecy wrongly label him as a racist, a hate teacher, or of being anti-white, and of teaching black supremacy.

But, this evening, we are all here at the Harvard Law School Forum together: both races, face to face. During the next few moments we can question and examine for ourselves the wisdom or the folly of what Mr. Muhammad is teaching.

Many of you who classify yourselves as "white" express surprise and shock at this truth that Mr. Muhammad is teaching among your 20 million ex-slaves here in America, but you should be neither surprised nor shocked.

As students, scholars, professors and scientists you should be well aware that we are living in a world and at a time when great changes are taking place. New ideas are replacing the old ones. Old governments are collapsing, and new nations are being born. The entire "old system" which has held the Old World together has lost its effectiveness, and now that Old World is going out. A new system or New World must replace the Old World.

Just as the old ideas must be removed to make way for the new, God has declared to Mr. Muhammad that the evil features of this wicked Old World must be exposed, faced up to, and removed in order to make way for the New World that God Himself is getting ready to establish.

The Divine Mission of Mr. Muhammad here in America today is to prepare us for this New World of Righteousness, by delivering to us a message that will give us a better understanding of this Old World's many defects . . .

and then we will all agree that God must remove this wicked Old World.

We see by reports in the daily press that even many of you who are scholars and scientists think that this message of Islam that is being taught here in America among your 20 million ex-slaves is "new," or that it is something Mr. Muhammad himself has made up.

Mr. Muhammad's religious message is not "new." All of the scientists and prophets of old predicted that a man such as he, with a doctrine or message such as this that Mr. Muhammad is spreading among your 20 million ex-slaves, would make his appearance among us at a time such as we are living in today.

It is also written in your own scriptures that this prophetic figure would not be raised up from the midst of the educated class, but that God would make His choice of a man from among the lowly, uneducated, downtrodden and oppressed masses . . . among the lowest element of America's 20 million ex-slaves.

Just as it was in the days when God raised up Moses from among the lowly Hebrew slaves, and missioned him to separate his oppressed people from a slave master named Pharaoh, and Moses found himself opposed by the scholars and scientists of that day, who are symbolically described in the bible as "Pharaoh's Magicians" . . .

And just as Jesus, himself a lowly carpenter, was also missioned by God in that day to find his people (the "lost sheep") and separate them from their Gentile enemies, and restore them back among their own people . . . Jesus also found himself opposed by the scholars and scientists of his day, who are symbolically described in the bible as "scribes, priests, and pharisees."

Just as the learned class of those days disagreed and opposed both Moses and Jesus primarily because of their humble origin and status, today Mr. Elijah Muhammad is likewise being opposed by the learned, educated intellectuals from among his own kind primarily because of his humble origin and status in their eyesight, and efforts are made by these modern-day "magicians, scribes, and Pharisees" to ridicule Mr. Muhammad by magnifying the humble origin of his many followers.

Moses was raised up among his enslaved people at a

time when God was planning to remove the power of the slave master and bring about a great change by placing the slaves in a land of their own where they could give birth to a "New Civilization," completely independent of their former slave master. Pharaoh opposed God's plan and God's servant, so Pharaoh and his people were destroyed.

Jesus was sent among his people again at a time when God was planning to bring about a great change. The new dispensation preached by Jesus 2,000 years ago ushered in a new type of civilization, the Christian civilization, better known as the Christian world.

The Holy Prophet Muhammad (may the peace and blessings of ALLAH be upon him) came 600 years after Jesus with another dispensation that did not destroy or remove the Christian civilization, but it did put a dent in it, a wound that has lasted even until today.

Now today, God has sent Mr. Elijah Muhammad among the downtrodden and oppressed so-called American Negroes to warn us that God is again about to bring about another great change . . . only this time, it will be a FINAL CHANGE! This is the day and the time for a COMPLETE CHANGE.

Mr. Muhammad is teaching that the religion of Islam is the only solution to the problems confronting our people here in America, but he also warns us that it is even more important for us to know the base or foundation of that which we must build upon tomorrow.

Therefore, the way in which Mr. Muhammad teaches us the religion of Islam, and the particular kind of Islam he teaches us, may appear to be different from that which is taught in the Old World of Islam, but the basic principles and practices are the same.

You must remember: the condition of America's 20 million ex-slaves is uniquely pitiful. But, just as the old religious leaders in the days of Moses and Jesus refused to accept Moses and Jesus as religious reformers, today many of the religious leaders in the Old Muslim World may also refute the teachings of Mr. Elijah Muhammad . . . not realizing the unique condition of these 20 million ex-slaves, and by not understanding that Mr. Elijah Muhammad's teachings are divinely prescribed to rectify the miserable condition of our oppressed people here . . . but

as God made Pharaoh's Magicians bow before Moses, and the Scribes and Pharisees bow before Jesus . . . it is God's plan today to make all opposition (both at home and abroad) bow before this truth that is now being taught by The Honorable Elijah Muhammad.

We are 4,000 years from the time of that great change which took place in Moses' day . . . we are 2,000 years from the time of that great change that took place in Jesus' day . . . and if you will but look around you on this earth today it will be as clear as the five fingers on your hand that we are again living at the time of a great change right now.

God has come to close out the entire Old World . . . the Old World in which for the past 6,000 years practically the entire earth has been deceived, conquered, colonized, ruled, enslaved, oppressed and exploited by the CAUCASIAN RACE.

When Pharaoh's civilization had reached its peak, and his time to rule over the slaves was up, God appeared unto Moses and revealed to him that He had something different for his people. Likewise, God has told Mr. Muhammad that He has something different for his People (the so-called Negroes) here in America today, something that up until now has never before been revealed . . . Mr. Muhammad teaches us that this Old World has seen nothing yet . . . the REAL THING is yet to come.

The Black Muslims who follow Mr. Muhammad are not only making our exit out of the door of the Old World, but the door to the New World is yet to be opened . . . and what is inside that door is yet to be revealed.

This present teaching of Mr. Muhammad among your 20 million ex-slaves is only to prepare us to walk out of this wicked Old World in as intelligent, pleasant, and peaceful a way as is possible.

This present teaching among the so-called American Negroes is designed only to show proof to us why we should give up this wicked Old House. The roof is leaking; the walls are collapsing, and we find it is no longer able to support the tremendous weight caused by our continued presence in it.

And since the knowledge of the deterioration and eventual collapse of this Old Building has come to Mr. Mu-

hammad from Almighty God Himself, whose proper name is ALLAH, the Lord of all the Worlds, the Master of the Judgment Day . . . The Honorable Elijah Muhammad is pointing these dangerous present conditions and future events out to you who have enslaved us, as well as to us.

With the proper support and guidance our people can get out of this sagging Old Building before it collapses.

But this support and guidance that we need actually consists of being taught: a thorough knowledge of the origin, history and nature of the Caucasian race, as well as a thorough knowledge of our own black nation. We must have a knowledge of the true origin and history and the white man's Christian religion, as well as an understanding of the Islamic religion that prevails primarily among our brothers and sisters in Africa and Asia.

You will probably ask us: Why then, if this Old House is going to collapse or go up in smoke, are the Black Muslims asking for some states to be set aside for us right here in this country . . . it's like asking for a chance to retain rooms in a house that you claim is doomed for total destruction?

God is giving America every opportunity to repent and atone for the crime she committed when she enslaved our people, just as God gave Pharaoh a chance to repent before He finally destroyed him because he was too proud to free his slaves and give them complete justice.

We are asking you for territory here only because of the great opposition we receive from this government in our efforts to awaken our people, unite them, separate them from their oppressors, and return them to our own land and people.

You should never make the drastic mistake of thinking that Mr. Muhammad has no place to take his followers in the World of Islam. No sir! He is not shut out there like many of you wish to believe. All who accept Islam and follow him have been offered a home in the Muslim World.

Our people have been oppressed and exploited here in America for 400 years, and now with Mr. Muhammad we can leave this wicked land of bondage, but our former slave master is yet opposing his efforts and is unjustly persecuting his followers who have left the Christian church and accepted the religion of Islam.

This is further proof that our Caucasian slave master does not want us or trust us to leave him and live elsewhere on this earth, and yet if we stay here among them he continues to keep us at the very lowest level of his society.

Pick up any daily paper or magazine and examine the anti-Muslim propaganda and the false charges leveled against our beloved religious leader by some of America's leading reporters. This only points up the fact that the Caucasian race is never willing to let any black man who is not their puppet or parrot speak for our people or lead our people out of their enslaving clutches without giving him great opposition.

The Caucasian slave master has opposed all such leaders in the past, and even today he sanctions and supports only those Negro spokesmen who parrot his doctrines, his ideas . . . or those who accept his so-called "advice" on how our people should carry on our struggle against his 400 years of tyranny.

The Christian world has failed to give the black man justice. This Christian government has failed to give 20 million ex-slaves justice for our 310 years of free slave labor. Despite this, we have been better Christians even than those who taught us Christianity. We have been America's most faithful servants during peace time, and her bravest soldiers during war time. And still, white Christians have been unable to recognize us and accept us as fellow human beings. Today we can see that the Christian religion of the Caucasian race has failed us. Thus the black masses are turning away from the church back to the religion of Islam.

The government sends its agents among our people to tell lies: they have a well-organized all-out effort to harass them, in an effort to frighten those of our people in this country who wish to accept the religion of Islam, and unite under the spiritual guidance and divine leadership of The Honorable Elijah Muhammad.

Therefore, Mr. Muhammad has declared to you, and to your government, that if you don't want your 20 million ex-slaves to leave you and return to our own land and people . . . and since your actions have proved that the Caucasian race will not accept these 20 million ex-slaves

here among them as complete equals . . . then let us separate ourselves from you right here, into a separate territory
that we can call our own, and on which we can do something for ourselves and for our own kind.

Since we cannot live among the Caucasians in peace,
and there is not enough time left for us (this new Negro)
to wait for the Caucasian race to be "re-educated" and
freed of their racial prejudices, and their inbred beliefs
and practices of white supremacy . . . I repeat: Let our
people be separated from you, and give us some territory
here that we can call our own, and live in peace among
ourselves.

According to recent news dispatches appearing in daily
papers throughout this nation: In prisons all over the country the wardens are unjustly persecuting the inmates who
want to change from the Christian religion and accept the
religion of Islam and follow the spiritual guidance of The
Honorable Elijah Muhammad.

These prison wardens even admit that when the inmates
change from Christianity to Islam they become model prisoners, but despite this they are being persecuted and prevented from reading the Holy Quran, the same Holy Book
that is read daily by hundreds of millions of our darker
brothers and sisters in Africa and Asia.

When the true facts about this religious persecution are
made known among the 725 million Muslims in the World
of Islam, that strategic area that stretches from the China
Seas to the shores of West Africa, how do you think the
American Caucasians will then look in the eyes of those
non-white people there?

The very fact that there is a concerted effort against
Islam by wardens across the country is proof that the
American government is trying to stamp out the religion
of Islam here in a frantic effort to keep it from spreading
among her 20 million ex-slaves whom she continues to con-
fine to the lowly role of second-class citizenship.

Further proof of this is the fact that these 20 million
so-called Negroes have never even been taught about the
religion of Islam during the entire 400 years since the
Caucasian first brought our people here away from our
African Muslim culture in chains . . . and despite the fact

that Islam is, and always has been, the prevailing religion among our people in Africa.

Now the American Caucasian, in a last act of desperation, is accusing Mr. Muhammad of not being a true Muslim, and of not teaching true Islam. If the American Caucasian knows so much about true Islam, and· has suddenly become such an authority on it, why hasn't he taught it to his 20 million ex-slaves before now?

Also, the American Caucasian today loves to print glaring headlines saying that the orthodox Muslims don't recognize or accept Mr. Muhammad and his Black Muslims as true Muslims.

"Divide and rule" has long been the Caucasian strategy to continue their colonization of dark people. The American Caucasian actually has colonized 20 million black people here in this country simply by dividing us from our African brothers and sisters for 400 years, converting us to his Christian religion, and then by teaching us to call ourselves "Negroes" . . . and telling us we were no longer African . . . (I guess he says this because our exposure to this "superior" white culture makes us "different" . . . so-called "civilized.")

As hundreds of thousands of the ex-slaves here in America today refuse to attend the church of the Caucasians who enslaved us, shunning all further use of the word "Negro," and because we are accepting ALLAH as our God, Islam as our religion, and The Honorable Elijah Muhammad as our religious leader and teacher . . . now the Americans who enslaved us are reverting back to the old trick of their fellow colonialists . . . "divide and rule" . . . by trying to separate us from the Muslim World, thinking that they can in this way alienate us from our people in Africa and Asia who also serve and follow Almighty God, ALLAH.

There are probably 100,000 of what you (whites) call orthodox Muslims in America, who were born in the Muslim World, and who willingly migrated here. But, despite the fact that Islam is a propagating religion, all of these foreign Muslims combined have not been successful in converting 1,000 Americans to Islam.

On the other hand, they see that Mr. Muhammad, all by himself, has hundreds of thousands of his fellow ex-

slaves turning Eastward toward Mecca five times daily giving praises to the Great God ALLAH.

No true Muslim, in his right mind, would denounce or deny this meek and humble little black man, who was himself born in Georgia, the very worst part of this country, as a leader, a defender of the faith, a propagator of the faith, who has rekindled the light of Islam here in the West.

His Caucasian opposers have never gotten even one responsible Muslim official to criticize or denounce Mr. Muhammad. They succeed only in getting some jealous or envious little peddler or merchant who migrated here and wants to be recognized as some sort of leader himself, and who will therefore accept the Caucasian's thirty pieces of silver to attack this man of God.

How would Mr. Muhammad ever make a trip into the forbidden areas of Arabia, and visit the Holy Cities of Mecca and Medina . . . being welcomed and honored by its most respected religious leaders . . . the great Imams themselves . . . if he himself was not recognized as a great religious man, and a man of God, doing miraculous works by spreading ALLAH's name here in the West among the 20 million ex-slaves of America?

How could Mr. Muhammad visit the capitals of the Muslim World, and be received by its respected leaders, if he too was not recognized and respected as a Muslim leader by them?

He visited Al-Azhar, the oldest Mosque and Muslim University in the world, and had tea with the Chief Imam, the Grand Sheikh Shaltuat, who kissed him on his forehead in true Muslim fashion . . . yet the American Caucasians, hoping to block his success among our people, continue to oppose him and say he is not a true Muslim.

Again you will say: Why then don't he and his followers leave this house of bondage right now, and go and live in the Muslim World? All of the Black Muslims can live in the Muslim World tomorrow, but The Honorable Elijah Muhammad wants justice for the entire 20 million so-called Negroes.

You and your Christian government make the problem even more complicated. You don't want your 20 million

ex-slaves to leave you, yet you won't share equal justice with them right here.

Since you don't want them to leave this country with us, and you won't give them equal justice among your kind . . . then we will agree only if you let us separate ourselves from you right here.

Just give us a portion of this country that we can call our own. Put us in it. Then give us everything we need to start our own civilization here . . . that is, support us for 20 to 25 years, until we are able to go for ourselves. This is God's plan. This is God's solution. This is justice, and compensation for our 310 years of free slave labor.

Otherwise America will reap the full fury of God's wrath, for her crimes against our people here are many. As your bible says: "He that leads into captivity shall go into captivity; he that kills with the sword shall be killed by the sword." This is the law of justice and this is in your own Christian scriptures.

The black masses are shaking off the drugs, or narcotic effect of the token integration promises. A cup of tea in a white restaurant is not sufficient compensation for 310 years of free slave labor. The black masses as represented by the Black Muslims will never be satisfied until we have some land that we can call our own.

Again I repeat: we are not asking for territory here because Mr. Muhammad has no place else to take us. But, to benefit the entire 20 million so-called Negroes, 20 million ex-slaves, who, despite the fact that the Emancipation Proclamation was issued 100 years ago. . . . These oppressed people are still begging their former slave master for recognition as human beings . . . therefore, Mr. Muhammad is asking this government to stop toying with our people, stop fooling them year in and year out with false promises of token integration.

Token integration will not solve our problem. This is a false solution. A "token" solution. It is a hypocritical approach to the problem, a tricky scheme devised by you, and propagated by your Negro puppets whom you yourself have appointed as our "leaders" and "spokesmen."

Integration is not good for either side. It will destroy your race, and your government knows it will also destroy ours . . . and the problem will still remain unsolved.

God has declared that these 20 million ex-slaves must have a home of their own. After 400 years here among the Caucasians, we are absolutely convinced that we can never live together in peace, unless we are willing to remain subservient to our former masters . . . therefore, immediate and complete separation is the only solution.

NAACP Attorney Thurgood Marshall has admitted publicly that six years since the Supreme Court decision on DESEGREGATION of the schools, only 6 per cent desegregation has taken place. This is an example of integration!

A kidnaper, a robber, an enslaver, a lyncher is just another common criminal in the sight of God, and the above-mentioned criminal acts have been committed on a mass scale for 400 years by your race against America's 20 million so-called Negroes.

It is true that today America professes to be sorry for her crimes against our people, and she says she wants to repent and in her desire to atone or make amends she offers her 20 million ex-slaves flowery promises of "token" integration.

Many of these downtrodden victims want to forgive America; they want to forget the crimes you have committed against them, and some are even willing to accept the formula of "token integration" that you yourself have devised as the solution to correct the problems created by your criminal acts against them.

In a court of justice the criminal can confess his crimes and throw himself on the mercy of the court if he has truly repented, but neither the criminal nor his victims have any say-so in suggesting the sentence that is to be passed upon the guilty . . . or the price that the confessed criminal must pay. This is left in the hands of the Judge. We are living in the Day of Judgment right now. God is the Judge that our American slave master must now answer to.

God is striking this great country with tornadoes, storms, floods, rain, hail, snow . . . and terrific earthquakes are yet to come. Your people are being afflicted with increasing epidemics of illness and disease, divine plagues that God is striking you with because of your criminal acts against the 20 million ex-slaves . . . and today instead of repenting and truly compensating our people for their 310 years of

free slave labor that built up this great country for you, you buy out the Negro leaders with 30 pieces of silver and get them to sell our people on accepting your "token integration."

When one uses a "token" on the bus or streetcar that "token" is a substitute for the real money. Token means "a substitute," that which takes the place of the real thing.

Token integration takes the place of the real thing. Two black students at Georgia University is TOKEN integration. Four black children in New Orleans white schools is TOKEN integration. A handful of black students in the white schools in Little Rock is TOKEN integration. None of this is REAL integration; it is only a pacifier designed to keep these awakening black babies from crying too loud.

The white man's violent rebellion, and relentless struggle against TOKEN integration is sufficient to prove what would happen if the Negro leaders demanded REAL INTEGRATION.

Also, according to the above-mentioned rate of speed since the desegregation decisions of the Supreme Court, it will take us another thousand years to get the white man in the South sufficiently "re-educated" to accept our people in their midst as equals . . . and if the rest of the truth is told, it will also take the white man here in the North, West and East just as long as his brother in the South . . . if the frightened Uncle Tom leadership ever stops accepting his master's "tokens" and begins to demand the real thing.

To many of you here at the Harvard Law School Forum this evening, this sounds ridiculous; to some it even sounds insane. But these 20 million black people here in America now number a nation in their own right. Do you believe a nation within another nation can be successful? Especially when they both have equal education?

Once the slave has his master's education, the slave wants to be like his master, wants to share his master's property, and even wants to exercise the same privileges as his master even while he is yet in his master's house.

This is the CORE of America's troubles today; and there will be no peace for America as long as 20 million so-called Negroes are here BEGGING for the rights which America knows she will never grant us.

Even this limited education America has granted her ex-slaves has already produced great unrest . . . and Al-

mighty God says the only way for America to ever have any future peace or prosperity is for her 20 million ex-slaves to be SEPARATED from her . . . and it is for this reason that Mr. Muhammad teaches us that we must have some land of our own.

If we receive equal education, how long do you expect us to remain your passive servants, or second-class citizens? There is no such thing as a second-class citizen. We are FULL CITIZENS or we are not citizens at all.

When you teach a man the science of government he wants an equal part (or position) in that government . . . or else he wants a government himself. He begins to demand equality with his master.

No man with equal education will serve you. The only way you can continue to rule us is with a superior knowledge, or by continuing to withhold equal education from our people.

America has not given us equal education, but she has given us enough to make us want more . . . and to make us demand equality of opportunity . . . and this is causing unrest . . . plus international embarrassment . . . thus the only solution is immediate SEPARATION.

As your colleges and universities turn out an ever increasing number of so-called Negro graduates with education equal to yours, they will automatically increase their demands for equality in EVERYTHING else. This equal education will increase their spirit of equality and make them feel that they should have EVERYTHING that you have, and their increasing demands will become a perpetual headache for you . . . and continue to cause you international embarrassment.

In fact, the same Negro students you are turning out today will soon be demanding the same things you now hear being demanded by Mr. Muhammad and the Black Muslims.

In my conclusion: I must remind you that since your own Christian bible states that God is coming in the "last days," or at the "end of the Old World," and that God's coming would bring about a GREAT SEPARATION . . . and since we see all sorts of signs throughout the earth that indicate that THE TIME OF GOD'S COMING is upon us . . . why don't you repent while there is yet time?

Do justice by your faithful ex-slaves. Give us some land of our own right here, some SEPARATE STATES, so we can separate ourselves from you . . . then everyone will be satisfied, and perhaps we will all be able to then live happily ever after, as your own Christian bible says . . . "every one under his own vine and fig tree."

Otherwise: all of you who are sitting here, your government, and your entire race will be destroyed and removed from this earth by Almighty God, ALLAH. I thank you.

3. MALCOLM X
ON "UNITY"

*Malcolm X delivered this speech at a so-called "unity" rally
on the streets of Harlem early in the spring of 1960. As the
text indicates, politics was in the air, and the Black Muslims
were calling for "unity" among Negro leaders.*

*The stage was set for the rally when the Black Muslims
telegraphed some fifteen outstanding Negro leaders, asking
them to participate in the affair. None of them came, but
this did not stop Malcolm X from unburdening himself.
Here again we see Malcolm X on the defensive, but in a
somewhat different way. In the first half of the speech
Malcolm is pulling in his horns; he is saying "unity," "freedom," "peace." He is suggesting a summit meeting of Negro
leaders. "Let's have our arguments behind closed doors,"
Malcolm shouts, "but let's come out unified."*

*At that juncture, however, nobody was willing to practice
summitry with the Black Muslims.*

*Malcolm used this speech to point up the Black Muslim
concern for morality; he attacks the dope, crime, and prostitution of Harlem as well as those—black and white—who
thrive upon these evils.*

*As expected, Malcolm concludes with the call for a sep-
arate state; he restates his Harvard offer: the white race can
be spared from destruction if they give the Negro a separate
state.*

*The rally lasted five hours; thirteen black nationalist groups
were represented, and some four thousand people blocked
off 125th Street and Seventh Avenue at the peak of the rally.*

AS-SALAAM-ALAIKUM, BELOVED BROTHERS AND SISTERS. WEL-
COME TO OUR HARLEM FREEDOM RALLY.

When we say "our" we do not mean Muslim nor Christian, Catholic nor Protestant, Baptist nor Methodist, Democrat nor Republican, Mason nor Elk. By "our" Harlem Freedom, we mean the black people of Harlem, the black people of America, and the black people all over this earth.

The largest concentration of black people on earth is right here in Harlem, so we are gathered here today in Harlem Square to a Freedom Rally, of black people, by black people, and for the benefit of black people.

We are not here at this Rally because we have already gained freedom. No! We are gathered here rallying for the freedom which we have long been promised, but have as yet not received. This Rally is for that perfect freedom which up until now this government has not granted us. There would be no need to protest to the government if we were already free.

Freedom is essential to life itself. Freedom is essential to the development of the human being. If we don't have freedom we can never expect justice and equality. Only after we have freedom do justice and equality become a reality.

Today we are gathered at this Rally to hear from our leaders who have been acting as our spokesmen, and representing us to the white man downtown. We want to know how our leaders really think, how they talk, how they feel . . . and most important of all, we want them to know how we feel.

Many of these leaders have suddenly become "experts on Harlem" and as such are often regarded by the white man as the "voice of Harlem." If this must be the case, then we want the voice of these leaders to ring sometimes in Harlem too.

Leaders have differences, and these differences ofttimes cause serious division among the masses. But the HOUR is too short today for black people to afford the luxury of "differences."

Again I repeat, we are not gathered here today because we are Muslims or Christians, Protestants or Catholics, Baptists or Methodists, Democrats or Republicans, Masons or Elks . . . but because as a collective mass of black people we have been colonized, enslaved, lynched, exploited, deceived, abused, etc.

As a collective mass of black people we have been deprived,

not only of civil rights, but even our human rights, the right to human dignity . . . the right to be a human being!

This Freedom Rally is to be a united effort by all our leaders. We have set aside all petty differences, and in the Spirit of Bandung we have come together on this same platform, wherein each one can voice his personal feelings and his personal solution to this grave crisis we face.

The Western World today faces a great catastrophe. It stands on the brink of disaster. Mr. Muhammad says the only way our people can avoid the fiery destruction that God Himself will soon unleash upon this wicked world is for our people to come together among themselves in unity and practice true brotherhood. Mr. Muhammad says God is with us to unite our people into one brotherhood, and to aid those that are oppressed, and to uplift those who are downtrodden.

The Western World, filled with evil and wickedness, is groping and stumbling blindly through spiritual darkness toward its inevitable doom. Mr. Muhammad says we must qualify ourselves so that God's spiritual light will guide us past the pitfalls of destruction.

The Western World is filled with drunkenness, dope addiction, lying, stealing, gambling, adultery, fornication, prostitution and hosts of other evils. These evils must be removed if the world is to have peace. These evils are the primary cause of troubles all over the earth. These evils promote greed and lust, increase wickedness and unrest, and destroy all hopes for peace.

You want peace. I want peace. Everyone craves for a world of peace. Mr. Muhammad says anyone who will submit to the God of Peace will have peace. Even the white man himself can prolong his time today if he will submit to the God of Peace, and give freedom, justice, and equality to the "people of God" . . . the so-called Negroes here in America.

The city of Nineveh in the bible to whom Jonah was sent to warn is a good prophetic example of today. They were actually spared because they repented when the warning came to them from God. God will spare our slave master today too if he will repent.

The whole dark world wants peace. When I was in Africa last year I was deeply impressed by the desire of our African Brothers for peace, but even they agree that there can be

no peace without freedom from colonialism, foreign domination, oppression and exploitation.

The God of Peace and Righteousness is about to set up His kingdom of peace and righteousness here on this earth. Knowing that God is about to establish His righteous government, Mr. Muhammad is trying to clean up our morals and qualify us to enter into this new righteous nation of God.

The American so-called Negroes must recognize each other as brothers and sisters . . . stop carrying guns and knives to harm each other, stop drinking whiskey, taking dope, reefers, and even cigarettes. No more gambling! Save your money. Stop fornication, adultery and prostitution. Elevate the black woman; respect her and protect her. Let us rid ourselves of immoral habits and God will be with us to protect and guide us.

Then, we must form a platform that will be good for all of our own people, as well as for others. As black people we must unite. We must recognize and give intelligent active support to our political leaders who fight for us unselfishly, sincerely, and fearlessly.

But, to prove their sincerity and their right for the support of the black masses, these leaders must first display fearlessness, intelligence, and unity among themselves. They must stop their public bickering with each other. They must stop attacking each other in front of the white man, and for the benefit of the white man.

If the black leaders must have differences of opinion, learn to go into the closet with each other, but when you come from behind closed doors, show a united front in the face of the one who is a common enemy to all of us.

Mr. Muhammad has invited all of the leaders here today for that purpose. He wants our people united, but unity will never exist among the black masses as long as our leaders are not united.

We want to get behind leaders who will fight for us . . . leaders who are not afraid to demand freedom, justice, and equality. We do not want leaders who are hand picked for us by the white man. We don't want any more Uncle Toms. We don't want any more leaders who are puppets or parrots for the white man.

We want brave leaders as our spokesmen, who are not

afraid to state our case, who can intelligently demand what
we need, what we want, and what is rightfully ours. We
don't want leaders who are beggars, who feel they must
compromise with the enemy. And we don't want leaders
who are selfish or greedy . . . who will sell us out for a few
pieces of silver.

A big election is coming up this year. What kind of leaders do we want in office? Which ones will the black masses
get behind? Mr. Muhammad has thousands of followers,
and millions of sympathizers. He will place his weight behind
any fearless black leaders who will stand up and help the
so-called American Negroes get complete and immediate freedom.

If these black leaders are afraid that to be identified with
us they will irk the white man, or lose the white man's
favor or his support, then they can no longer expect the support of the black masses.

They call us racial extremists. They call Jomo Kenyatta
also a racial extremist and Tom Mboya a moderate. It is
only the white man's fear of men like Kenyatta that makes
him listen to men like Mboya. If it were not for the extremists, the white man would ignore the moderates. To
be called a "moderate" in this awakening dark world today,
that is crying for freedom, is to receive the "kiss of death"
as spokesmen or leaders of the masses . . . for the masses
are ready to burst the shackles of slavery whether the "moderates" will stand up or not.

We have many black leaders who are unafraid, especially
when they know the black masses stand behind them. Many
of them are qualified to represent us not only in this United
States government, but could also represent us in this government if we are given 100 per cent citizenship and the opportunity for FIRST-CLASS participation . . . or else we can
get behind these same leaders in setting up an independent
government of our own.

We, the black masses, don't want these leaders who seek
our support coming to us representing a certain political
party. They must come to us today as black leaders representing the welfare of black people.

We won't follow any leader today who comes on the basis
of political party. Both parties (Democrat and Republican)
are controlled by the same people who have abused our

rights, and who have deceived us with false promises every time an election rolls around.

Mr. Muhammad grieves over the disunity that exists even among the intellectuals and professional so-called Negroes. It is these "educated" so-called Negroes who should be leading us out of this maze of misery and want. They possess the academic know-how, great amounts of technical skills . . . but they can't use it for the benefit of their own kind simply because they themselves are also disunited. If these intellectuals and professional so-called Negroes would unite, not only Harlem would benefit, but it will benefit our people all over the world.

Mr. Muhammad says disunity is our number one stumbling block, and this disunity exists only because we lack knowledge of SELF (our own kind). So-called Negro "intellectuals" seem to think integration is the answer. But, is it? "Integrate" means to become as one unit. How can these "intellectuals" expect the white man to accept us into his social unit, political unit, or economic unit when we are not yet in unity (as a unit) among our own kind?

We, the Muslims, are for "Brotherhood," but not for integration! What is the difference? Brotherhood is based on love, which automatically produces voluntary acts of "sincere benevolence." But integration produces hypocrisy. It forces the white man to pose as a "liberal," to be pretensive and false. Thus, "benevolent" acts which are "forced by integration laws" are producing white hypocrites, and reducing chances of creating a "mutual-working-agreement" between the two races.

Your thirst for integration makes the white man think you want only to marry his daughter. We (Muslims) who follow Mr. Muhammad don't think God ever intended for black men to marry white women. Mr. Muhammad and his followers are violently opposed to intermarriage.

This is conveniently and purposely misinterpreted by our enemies to mean that we are anti-white, anti-Christian, and anti-American (simply because we refuse to chase after the white man's women!). Let the white man keep his women, and let us keep ours.

Some Negroes who love race-mixing, and want white women, are angry at Mr. Muhammad because he teaches against race-mixing . . . so they slip around and make the

white man think we are anti-white. (I'm surprised that the white man is dumb enough to believe these Uncle Toms, who stoop so low, like JUDAS, to be stool pigeons against their own kind.)

We have oceans of dark people on this earth: in Africa, Asia, and even here in America. Our women are the most beautiful, like a bouquet of flowers. Why should we chase white women?

In this "changing" world today, what would we do married to a white woman? Her people don't want you in their neighborhood around them, and our fast awakening people don't want you to bring her back into our neighborhood any more to live around us. Thus, you both become a "misfit" . . . unwelcomed and unwanted in either society . . . where can you go?

Because we Muslims look at this as it is and face reality does not mean we are anti-white. We don't want his white mother, his white sister, nor his white daughter. We want only an equal chance on this earth, but to have an equal chance we must have the same thing the white man himself needed before he could get this nation started . . . WE MUST HAVE SOME LAND OF OUR OWN!

Why do we want some land of our own? Because land is essential to freedom. How else can 20 million black people who now constitute a nation in our own right, a NATION WITHIN A NATION, expect to survive forever in a land where we are the last ones hired and the first ones fired . . . simply because we have no land of our own?

For over 400 years we have been very faithful to our American slave masters. Now God is warning them through Mr. Muhammad that they should be nice enough to give us some land so we can separate ourselves from them and get started for ourselves.

This is no more than what the white man should do. It is in complete accord with the Christian religion. Their bible says that when a slave is set free, his slave master should give him something to help him get started on his own . . . never send him away empty-handed.

If the Hebrews in the Bible numbered only 600,000 in the land of their bondage, and God was concerned with giving them freedom in a land of their own, a land "flowing with milk and honey" . . . then what about 20 million so-

called Negroes here in America, who have the "freedom" only to look for a job?

Can you not see that our former "leaders" have been fighting for the wrong thing . . . the wrong kind of freedom? Mr. Muhammad says we must have some land where we can work hard for ourselves, make ourselves equal, and live in dignity. Then and only then we won't have to beg the white man for the crumbs that fall occasionally from his table. No one respects or appreciates a beggar.

Since we say Lincoln freed us, let us avail ourselves of that freedom by uniting together and doing something for our own kind. But, we must have some of this earth. We have been in America over 400 years. We have been so-called "free" 100 years, and yet he still calls us "the white man's burden."

We Muslims don't want to be a burden on America any longer. God has given Mr. Muhammad a divine message, program, and solution. WE MUST HAVE SOME LAND! The white man should be glad to give his loyal "slaves" some land so we can get out of his way and go for ourselves.

We will then set up our own farms, factories, business, and schools . . . and show him how much we appreciate the education he has given us, by using it to become self-sustaining . . . economically and otherwise.

We want some land where we can create unity, harmony and brotherhood . . . and live together in peace. Since America now sees that this false show of integration and intermarriage will not work, she should make immediate steps to set aside a few of these states for us, and put us there to ourselves.

If America will repent and do this, God will overlook some of our wicked deeds (as in the days of Nineveh) . . . but if America refuses to give Mr. Muhammad what God instructed him to ask for . . . then, like the biblical houses of Egypt and Babylon (slave empires of the bible), God will erase the American government and the entire race that it favors and represents, from this planet . . . and God will then give the whole earth back to the original owners, the black man!

4. MALCOLM X's
"UNIVERSITY SPEECH"

The following is Malcolm X's "university speech," a long lecture he used in the hope of converting students—particularly Negroes—on various university campuses during 1961-1962. It is of some interest that this speech was given at Atlanta University, the great citadel of Negro learning in the Deep South, and Dr. Lonnie Cross, chairman of the department of mathematics, not only joined the movement but became assistant to Jeremiah X, minister of the Atlanta Temple.

This lecture contains a unique passage. It will be recalled that in his Harvard speech Malcolm chastised Moslems from the East who had migrated to America but failed to gather converts. In this speech he goes further; in a stinging passage Malcolm flatly accuses Moslems from the East of attempting to turn "our slave masters" (the American white man) into good Moslems. He accuses orthodox Moslems of "passing us by" and attempting to proselytize the foes of the Negro rather than the Negro himself.

This is without doubt the strongest position any Muslim has ever taken against the orthodox Moslem movement and further underscores my contention that the Black Muslims are not really concerned about orthodox Islam. They need the façade of world-wide Islam, of course, but the Black Muslim movement is a home-grown operation with home-grown aims and ideas. Nowhere is that more clearly stated than in this "university speech."

ISLAM, the natural religion of black mankind, is sweeping through and resurrecting black America like a "flaming

136

fire," under the Divine Guidance of Messenger Elijah Muhammad.

Fools try to ignore facts, but wise men must face facts to remain wise. Fools refuse to change from their silly ways and beliefs, but the mental powers of the wise man encourage mental flexibility and enable him to keep an OPEN MIND. This gives him the ability to re-adjust himself whenever it becomes necessary for a CHANGE.

As fast as added "light" increases the wise man's ability to understand, he changes his "course" or his "pace" according to the newly revealed facts before him.

Fools, however, just blunder on, blindly, heedless of the ever-changing conditions on the road over which they must travel . . . thus, the BLIND DRIVERS and their "cars" usually end up in the DITCH.

In the past, the "religious roads" leading through black America presented smooth sailing for the "Old Touring Cars" (Churches) of Christianity. They met few obstacles and had little opposition or competition. The "drivers" (preachers) had it easy. Their "course" was never challenged. They ruled supreme on the religious roads of black America.

However, today time is making a great CHANGE. The religious roads of black America have suddenly become blocked by a ROCKY BARRIER, and all the black and white preachers combined are incapable of removing it. The firm, down-to-earth, thought-provoking teachings of the religion of Islam are now obstructing this path over which it was once easy sailing for these preachers of white man's Christianity.

Islam poses both a challenge and a threat because Islam is the "resurrecting power." Thousands of so-called Negroes are beginning for the first time to think for themselves, since turning away from the segregated Christian church, and are rejoining the ranks of their black brothers and sisters of the East. Their age-old faith is the religion of Islam, the religion of our foreparents, the true religion of black mankind.

The Spiritual Leader and Teacher of the many thousands of "New Believers" here in black America is Messenger Elijah Muhammad.

Before we heard the teachings of Messenger Muhammad, we (American so-called Negroes) were in the grave of

ignorance. We had been taught by our Christian slave master, as well as by our own ignorant religious leaders, that God had cursed us black and sentenced us to a lifetime of servitude to the Christian white race.

The same slave master's Christian religion promised us that we (Negroes) would sprout wings after death and fly up into the sky where God would have a place especially prepared for us.

Since we poor "cursed" slaves were not to get anything on earth while we were alive, we soon learned to expect it only after death, "up in the sky." Thus, this earth, and all its vast riches which we ourselves originally owned, was left to the deceitful maneuverings of the white race, for them to build a heaven for themselves and their own kind "in THIS life."

Such religious teachings were purposely designed to make us (so-called Negroes) feel inferior to the white Christian slave master. Soon he was successful in making us fear him, obey him, and worship him . . . instead of the true Supreme Being, the God of our own foreparents, Almighty God, ALLAH.

Messenger Muhammad has taught us how we eventually became like the beggar Lazarus of the bible (Luke 16:20): Our condition became very sore. We sat here amid the rubbish of the Western World, at the feet of the rich, white Christians . . . begging for the crumbs (civil rights and token integration) to fall from their table. But from this very same slave master whom our foreparents had made rich, by giving freely of their slave labor for nearly 400 years (Gen. 15:13), we received only the hardest and dirtiest jobs at the lowest wages; the poorest houses in the ghettos at the highest rent; the poorest food and clothing at the highest prices. Our schools were like shacks, and were staffed by teachers who knew and could teach only that which the slave master dictated to them.

Messenger Muhammad has taught us how we (so-called Negroes) were kidnaped from the East by the white Christian slave master, brought to America in chains, and robbed of our own God, His religion, our language, culture, names, flag, and even our own nationality. After robbing us of all that we originally could proudly call our own, then the slave master taught us to call ourselves "Negroes." He told us that

we were to be called "Negroes" because he found us along the banks of the Niger River.

Messenger Muhammad asks us today: "Since when does one's nationality originate from a river?" This same slave master taught us that "negro" means "black" in Spanish. Messenger Muhammad again asks us why, then, do not the dark, Spanish-speaking people in Spain, South and Central America accept it (Negro) as their nationality too? Messenger Muhammad says that we too should get our NATIONality from the NATION that our foreparents originated (as do all other recognized peoples).

The bible speaks of how we were purposely cut off from our own kind after being robbed of our identity by the cruel Christian slave master (Ezekiel 37:11; Psalms 137:1-9; 83:4). The slave master then took our names, language, and religion from us so we would have to accept his, obey him, and worship him (Dan. 1:6-7).

Messenger Muhammad has given us many scriptures to prove his teachings to us are true and in accord with the prophecies of the bible. He says it is we (so-called Negroes) in America who were robbed and made deaf, dumb, and blind to the knowledge of our own God and of our own selves; so that today we are like DRY BONES IN THE VALLEY (spiritually dead, and in a mental grave of ignorance).

We are now able to speak only the slave master's tongue, and are still being called the same "slave names" given to our fathers during slavery by the slave master . . . names such as Jones, Smith, Powell, King, Bunche, Diggs, Dawson, etc. These are all SLAVE NAMES, names of the very same slave master who has shown characteristics of his beast-like nature in his treatment of us. The original names of our foreparents were cut off from them, kept secret from us by the "beast" (Rev. 15:2), and therefore today we do not know what our real names should be. We have really been robbed!

All other people have their own religion, which teaches them of a God with whom they themselves can associate. A God who at least looks like one of their own kind. But, we (so-called Negroes), after 400 years of masterful brainwashing by the slave master, picture our "god" with the

·same blond hair, pale skin, and cold blue eyes of our murderous slave master.

His Christian religion teaches us that black is a curse; thus, we who accepted the slave master's religion found ourselves loving and respecting everything and everyone except black, and could picture God as being anything else but BLACK. In fact, many so-called Negroes would rather believe that God is INVISIBLE, a "colorless spirit," than to admit even the possibility of his being black. Yet Daniel saw Him with kinky hair (like lamb's wool) in the seventh chapter of Daniel, ninth verse. How grossly deceived we have been!

Messenger Muhammad says that the teachers and religious leaders of our own kind here in America were as blind to the REAL TRUTH as we; therefore, they themselves were not even qualified to lead us beyond that which the slave master had falsely taught them. HOW CAN THE BLIND LEAD THE BLIND? Thus, we remained in the DITCH (the GRAVE of spiritual ignorance, mental bondage) which was dug for us to fall into by our white Christian slave master.

Not only did our own preachers and educators here fail to give us the truth, our darker brothers who were born in the East came here from the East and neglected to convert us back to the original religion (ISLAM) of our foreparents. Many of our brothers from the East even failed to recognize us as their long-lost brothers ("lost sheep") who had been kidnaped from the Nation of Islam 400 years ago, and made to dwell here in this strange land, among these wicked people who are not of our own kind (Gen. 15:13), nor of our own choice.

Our brothers from the East passed us by, and instead, tried to lecture on Islam to our slave master, thinking, so foolishly, that they would be able to turn the slave master into a righteous Muslim . . . knowing all the time that the same slave master was the very one who had kidnaped, robbed, enslaved, and lynched (murdered) their long-lost brothers. Yes, our brothers from the East came here and seemed to be apologists for Islam, instead of rightly spreading it, or defending it from the sly insults of the unbelieving slave master.

Messenger Muhammad teaches us that Almighty God,

ALLAH, is all-powerful and independent. ALLAH needs no one to apologize for Him. Islam, His True Religion, is not a religion of compromise. Islam is truth itself, and this truth has long been kept a secret from us.

For 400 years, we (so-called Negroes) were deprived of Islam (life) by our white slave master, who in turn indoctrinated (brainwashed) us with his false religion of Christianity . . . and like the biblical Lazarus, we soon became so dead mentally and spiritually, that our attitude (disposition) became offensive (stank) in the nostrils of the intelligent and civilized world. Our kind in the East failed to recognize us as their long-lost brothers (the lost sheep). Our people in the East forgot us completely, and we, too, soon forgot our blood-ties with them.

But Almighty God ALLAH forgets not. As He promised in the Old Testament (Mal. 4:5) that He would send ELIJAH to the "lost sheep" (the so-called Negroes of America) in the "last days" (of the white man's world), to teach us the truth that would free us from our white slave master, and turn our hearts and minds back toward our own kind (our fathers in the East). And, in the last days of this wicked world, the hearts of our people in the East would be turned once again toward us (Isaiah 43:5).

We who have been raised by ELIJAH from the "grave" that was dug for us by the slave master, bear witness that this same ELIJAH, who was predicted to come, has been raised from our midst today and is even now with us here in America in the person of The Honorable Elijah Muhammad. He is the "first begotten" from this grave of ignorance, from the midst of we (so-called Negroes) who have long been a mentally dead people. He is the "First Fruit" raised from us who slept, and he has been raised from this grave by Almighty God, ALLAH Himself.

Examine his works among us, for his works are sufficient testimony to his identity. Only a fool, or an envious person, would fail to see the greatness of this man after examining his work. We who have been raised from the grave by him bear witness of his work.

In a short time, Messenger Muhammad is accomplishing what our educators and religious leaders here failed to do for 100 years, and what our brothers from the East neglected to do. Messenger Muhammad has brought our minds

out of the sky (where the ignorant preachers had sent it), and has made us better able to face the reality of living. He has restored life (truth) to our long-lost dead people. Who else other than Almighty God, ALLAH, could have given Messenger Muhammad the power to do what all others have failed to do?

"And Allah sent down WATER from above, and therewith gives life to the dead earth after its death. Surely there is a SIGN in this for a people who listen." (Quran 16:65.)

Praise be to ALLAH! Who would have believed it? An ex-slave, a man like Moses (Deut. 18:18), to whom ALLAH has given sufficient power to stand up and speak the truth so boldly here in the land of our bondage, facing not only the wrath of the wicked slave master (modern Pharaoh), but also the wrath of his own kind, who are ignorant of the truth. They are too blind to see what is good for them. There are those also who are jealous and envious of his Wisdom and his Divine Mission.

Messenger Muhammad's teachings have really inspired us with a thirst today for truth. We who follow him are filled with an enthusiastic desire to wear the Crown of Life, the jewels of which are: Wisdom, Knowledge, Understanding . . . Freedom, Justice, Equality . . . Food, Clothing, Shelter . . . and Love, Peace, and Happiness. He teaches us that these must be enjoyed while we are living.

These are the very essentials of life, and they adorn the Crown of Life which we shall all wear in ALLAH's Paradise, the Kingdom of God, which shall soon be set up on this earth, for us to enjoy while we are living.

Almighty God, ALLAH, has a religion of life, not of death, that teaches us to live, the importance of living, and how to live. ALLAH is the God of the living, and not the God of the dead.

All praise is due to ALLAH! We who once followed foolishly and blindly after the slave master's plurality of gods (TRINITY) and sought to have our heaven (the necessities of life) up in the sky after we die, are no longer fooled today by the slave master's lies. Today, we know there is but ONE GOD. There is no God but ALLAH! And, we bear witness that The Honorable Elijah Muhammad is His last and greatest Messenger to us here in North America.

Yes, we who were once dead (mentally, morally, socially,

politically, and economically), lying at the rich white man's feet here in the grave of ignorance, are being raised today from this "death." We are being made upright . . . PERPENDICULAR . . . by the WORD of this Noble Messenger of Almighty God, ALLAH. He has the Message of Life for 20,000,000 so-called Negroes here in America.

The people (Negroes) that walked in darkness (ignorance) have seen a great light (Islam): they that dwell in the land (of bondage) in the shadow of death (the Cross) upon them has the light shined (Isaiah 9:2).

Examine our previous condition, then judge Messenger Muhammad according to his work among us. We who are striving to carry his teachings into practice today are well on the road to mental, moral and financial independence.

Thanks to His Message we are well aware today of the importance of Freedom, Justice, Equality . . . Wisdom, Knowledge, Understanding . . . Food, Clothing, Shelter . . . Love, Peace and Happiness, in sufficient quantity and quality, while we are living, This great teacher has filled us with a desire to rest not, until we have our own righteous nation, united together under ALLAH, the One God, wherein brotherhood is a practiced reality instead of a future dream or a "far-away promise" as it is in the Christian religion of our slave master.

Even you must bear witness that Messenger Muhammad is without question the most fearless and uncompromising representative of Almighty God, ALLAH, and His Religion of Islam. Messenger Muhammad doesn't offer any apology to this wicked race, nor to the fearful and unbelieving "Uncle Toms" among our own kind. He has a Message from God. It is a warning of condemnation of the wicked, and despite all opposition he goes right ahead, boldly delivering his message.

He says (as Noah, Lot, and Moses did before him) that you can take it or leave it. So many of you will say that you believe in Almighty God, ALLAH; but, yet you hesitate to teach the naked truth, for fear of hurting the tender feelings of this wicked white race. Since you are filled with fear of the beast (Rev. 21:8), instead of standing in the way, holding up progress, hardening your hearts with envy, jealousy, and unbelief . . . step out of his way so he can prove to the world that there is no God but ALLAH, and

that this Great God ALLAH has come to redeem His long-lost people . . . the so-called Negroes of America (Rev. 7:2).

According to the bible, destruction of the slave master by Almighty God can no longer be avoided nor delayed. And, oh how well the slave master (modern Pharaoh) knows this. Yes, this government, which was founded upon the slavery and suffering of God's "chosen people," is quite upset today because of the teachings of Messenger Muhammad (the modern Moses), the same as the biblical Pharaoh was.

Government agents have visited and questioned me so persistently and thoroughly that I spent many a sleepless night wondering what it is about the presence of this little meek and humble man that has them so terribly concerned and upset.

Yes, they visited and questioned many of his followers, but the more they visit and question us the more clearly we are able to see and know that this is indeed a Divine Man, God-sent to us poor slaves (Exodus 3:6-10), with truth that forever frees us from fear of this wicked, modern Pharaoh.

This little black man has not been to college; his formal education in the slave master's school system is very limited, and he is not eloquent in his speech (Ex. 4:10), whereas these government agents who question us are highly trained and well schooled in all the modern sciences of life. They are well learned, yet the teachings of this little "unlearned" man has them hurt, confused, and upset. The average unlearned man cannot upset a learned person . . . unless he has been given something by the MOST LEARNED ONE, the All-Knowing One, Almighty God, ALLAH Himself.

All praise is due to ALLAH! How well He has enabled us to see that this little meek and humble man is he of whom the bible says: "How knoweth this man letters (such great wisdom) having never learned (being unlearned) . . ." (John 7:15). No man in history has ever fit such a prophetic picture more perfectly than this little "unlearned" man who is teaching us today with such great authority.

Yes, he may be "unlearned" according to the educational standards of the slave master, but he has been well schooled

by Almighty God, ALLAH Himself . . . for he tells us constantly that his doctrine (message) is not his own but was authored by the One God, ALLAH, who sent him (John 7:15).

All praise is due ALLAH! A man born in Georgia, mentally blind, deaf, and dumb, as ignorant as all the rest of us. Yet we see him today upsetting the slave master's health, just as biblical Moses did in ancient times to the slave master of that day (Ex. 5:2), simply by declaring God's plan to give these poor slaves (America's so-called Negroes) a land of our own, wherein we won't have to beg any slave master any more for "civil rights," for we shall then have in our own land a righteous government, wherein FREEDOM, JUSTICE, and EQUALITY and all the other essentials of life will be natural products, flowing for us and to us . . . like "milk and honey."

In the Holy Quran it says: "He it is who raised from among the ILLITERATES a Messenger from among themselves, who recites to them the book and the wisdom . . . although they were before in manifest error." (62:2.)

Also, "Those who follow the Messenger-Prophet, the ILLITERATE ONE, whom they find in the Torah and the Gospel. He enjoins them good, and forbids them evil, and makes lawful to them good things and prohibits for them impure things, and removes from them their burden and the shackles which were on them. So those who believe in Him and help Him, these are the successful." (7:157.)

I, myself, being one who was lost and dead, buried here in the rubbish of the West, in the thickest darkness of sin and ignorance, hoodwinked completely by the false teaching of the slave master, am able to stand upright today, PERPENDICULAR, on the square with my God, ALLAH, and my own kind (in the East) . . . able for the first time in 400 years to SEE and HEAR.

I bear witness that Almighty God, ALLAH, is the Finder of the lost sheep (American Negroes) and the Life-Giver to the dead. He, ALLAH, is the only Saviour for the 20,000,000 so-called Negroes, who were kidnaped by the white race and enslaved here in America.

Also, I bear witness that Messenger Elijah Muhammad has been taught (raised) by this Great God of the Universe,

the Architect of the Universe, the Supreme Being Himself, ALLAH. And I bear witness that Messenger Elijah Muhammad is in turn raising us from the dead today, teaching us TRUTH, and raising us from the dead level of ignorance.

5. MALCOLM X AT QUEENS COLLEGE

Mr. Muhammad Speaks *is the official newspaper of the Black Muslim movement. It is a highly charged, well-edited propaganda sheet of some thirty-six pages. One recent edition carried the full text of a speech Malcolm X delivered at Queens College in New York. More interesting than the speech—at least I feel so—is the way the editors of the paper led into the text. Here is a clear example of how Black Muslims are informed about what their leaders are doing. The paper had a circulation of over fifty thousand a year ago, and I suspect it has all but doubled that now. The picture painted here is that of their second-in-command, Malcolm X, issuing words of wisdom in the places of higher learning. Of particular interest is the description of students skipping class to question Malcolm.*

I was not at Queens College, but I have been with Malcolm —most of the time to debate with him—at other universities. And I know this scene to be valid. Whether people believe Malcolm X is one thing, but there can be no doubt that they come in droves—particularly white people—to hear him. And they always linger to ask questions.

New York Minister Malcolm X continued his series of successful presentations of the teachings of the Honorable Elijah Muhammad in Boston, St. Louis and New York, during the past few weeks.

On Tuesday, May 24th, Malcolm X spoke at the Boston Theological Seminary in Boston, Mass. The prior week Malcolm X was heard by several hundred St. Louis Negroes who jammed Carpenter's Hall, where Malcolm X said, "America must give Negroes full free-

dom or face disaster." Malcolm went on to say that complete and total separation resulting in the Negro having a few states of his own is the only solution to the so-called Negro problem.

Upwards of two hundred students [gathered] in room one hundred of the Remsen Building at New York's Queens College last month to hear Minister Malcolm X, head of Muhammad Temple of Islam Number Seven, defend the doctrine of Islam as taught by the Honorable Elijah Muhammad.

The students gathered at the invitation of the Queens College Chapter of the NAACP and heard Minister Malcolm say, "the American black man faces a unique situation because of his unique position in America. This is why so many American black men are turning to Islam and also why Islam must be presented to them in a form peculiar to the circumstances they face. This causes many people to say we are not teaching the orthodox form of Islam." Minister Malcolm continued, "This is not true. We are teaching the true Islamic faith but we are making it applicable to the peculiar conditions faced by the American black man."

Asked to comment on Mr. Muhammad's twelve point program for the salvation of the American Negro, Minister Malcolm said, "our central teaching as far as the social action of the American black man is concerned is that he should be separated from his slave masters. As the Bible says, 'let every man be under his own vine and fig tree.' Mr. Muhammad teaches that the American black man, like the children of Israel, are strangers, not in a land of their own."

"Much of the unrest now current would be eliminated," Minister Malcolm said, "if the request of Mr. Muhammad were granted. Once the slave is educated he wants to be equal with his master, to share his master's property. If the slave is as well educated as the master then the slave will no longer be content to serve. That is the core of the racial unrest in America today. That is why we must be separated and allowed to become a people self-sufficient and self-supporting."

The appearance of Minister Malcolm was scheduled to last for fifty-five minutes but the interest was such

that scores of students remained out of classes to continue discussions with Minister Malcolm for an hour past the stated deadline.

The following is a complete transcript of Minister Malcolm's Queens College speech:

WE THANK YOU for inviting us here today to present our views on this topic: "The Negro's Position in the Recent American Society." But, to understand our views you must first know something about our religion, Islam.

The Creator of the Universe, whom many of you call God or Jehovah, is known to the Muslims by the name ALLAH. Since the Muslims believe all prophets came from that ONE GOD and therefore all taught one and the same religion, rightly called ISLAM, which means the complete submission and obedience to ALLAH.

One who practices this Divine Obedience is called a Muslim (commonly known, spelled, and referred to here in the West as Moslem).

There are over 600 million Muslims on this earth, predominantly in Africa and Asia, and we here in America under the Divine Guidance of Mr. Elijah Muhammad are an integral part of the vast World of Islam that stretches from the China Seas to the sunny shores of West Africa.

A unique situation faces the black man here in America because of his unique condition, thus his acceptance of Islam and into Islam affects him uniquely . . . differently than all other converts of Islam.

Mr. Elijah Muhammad is our Divine Leader and Teacher here in America. He believes in and obeys God 100 per cent and is teaching and working among us to fulfill God's Divine Purpose.

What is this purpose? God's purpose today (just as it was in biblical days) is the complete SEPARATION of the so-called Negroes from their slave master . . . as the bible says concerning today: "Let every man be under his own vine and fig tree."

The best biblical example of this is the enslavement of the Hebrews in the land of Egypt under Pharaoh . . . a free man and some slaves who were "strangers in a land not their own," and how Jehovah chose Moses to SEPARATE them from their slave master.

Since the slave master today declares his "former" slaves are free, Mr. Muhammad says that for the betterment of our future and that of our former slave master God has declared we also must be SEPARATED.

To many of you here in this college auditorium, this sounds ridiculous; to some it even sounds insane. But 20 million black people here in America now number a nation in their own right. Do you believe a nation WITHIN another nation can be successful? Especially when they both have equal education?

Once the slave has his master's education, the slave wants to be like his master, wants to share his master's property, and wants to exercise the same privileges as his master.

This is the CORE of America's troubles today; and there will be no peace for America as long as 20 million so-called Negroes are here BEGGING for the equal rights which America knows she will never grant us.

Even the limited education America has granted her ex-slaves has already produced great unrest . . . and Almighty God says the only way for America to ever have peace is for us to be SEPARATED from her . . . and therefore Mr. Muhammad teaches us that we must have some land of our own.

If we receive equal education, how long do you expect us to remain your passive servants, or second-class citizens? There is no such thing as second-class citizens. We are FULL CITIZENS or we are not citizens at all!

When you teach a man the science of government he wants an equal part (or position) in that government . . . or else he wants to be a master in that government himself. He demands equality with his master.

No man with equal education will serve you. The only way you can continue to rule us is with a superior knowledge, or by continuing to hold equal education from our people.

America has not given us equal education, but she has given us enough to make us want more . . . and to make us demand equality of opportunity . . . which is causing great unrest.

Thus, the only SOLUTION is complete SEPARATION!

You believe in the fulfillment of biblical prophecy, that a great DAY OF SEPARATION is coming, and that the

knowledge of truth will cause this SEPARATION. We are living at that time today!

You are not common people here in this college audience. You are students, scholars, professors; you have education enough to weigh current events as well as history against the truth of what Mr. Muhammad is teaching.

For over 300 years our parents served yours. During slavery our parents didn't ask your parents for civil rights. Our parents did not have enough education to do so.

They were taught by their educated white masters that they were born inferiors . . . born to serve the whites . . . "superior" whites who restricted them without citizenship even after the so-called emancipation proclamation.

Today Mr. Muhammad sees nothing but the DESTRUC-TION of both races if they stay together. INTEGRATION will cause DISINTEGRATION of both.

A child stays within the mother until the time of birth. When the time of birth arrives, the child must be SEP-ARATED, or it will DESTROY its mother and itself. The mother can't carry that child after its time.

The child wants to be free; it cries for a world of its own. If the mother will not give it up NATURALLY, the doctors must forcibly take it from her . . . which sometimes causes her death.

If she can set it free naturally and easily, so much the better . . . if not, it must be TAKEN.

Twenty million so-called Negroes in America today num-ber a nation WITHIN a nation and are crying for FREE-DOM. We must be freed. We must be born. We must be SEPARATED . . . or cause the DESTRUCTION of both!

SEPARATION is the only solution today. Is this insane? Is this so ridiculous?

During slavery our parents would have been put to death for advocating integration with the white man . . . and now that God has declared this is the DAY OF SEPARATION, the white man wants (or at least is TALKING about) in-tegration with his ex-slave.

America can solve her present problems and avoid a worse crisis by setting up some SEPARATE STATES for us right here in America.

Remember the Hebrews in biblical Egypt . . . after their 400 years of bondage to Pharaoh were up, God had to ful-

fill his promise to them that he had made through Abraham
. . . but their biblical slave master would not let them go.

Thus it cost the slave master his own freedom, his country, and his life for opposing God's Plan to SEPARATE His
people from their slave master and set them in a land of
their own.

God would not have DESTROYED the slave master if
he would have listened . . . but just as America is today,
the biblical slave master (Pharaoh) was also too rich, too
strong, and too proud to listen to Moses . . . whom they
contemptuously looked upon only as an inarticulate ex-slave.

Mr. Muhammad is opposed today, both by his own people
and by whites, simply because he advocates complete FREE-
DOM, JUSTICE and EQUALITY for America's 20 million
so-called Negroes.

America is a free nation. Why should America oppose
Mr. Muhammad for teaching FREEDOM for her 20 million
so-called Negroes?

He is not asking for an "integrated society" which would
only lead to the dreaded INTERMARRIAGE with America's
white sons and daughters . . . he is demanding complete
SEPARATION where we will have complete FREEDOM,
JUSTICE, and EQUALITY in a land of our own.

And, if God is with Mr. Muhammad today to SEPARATE
us and put us in a land wherein we can form our own nation
equal with other civilized nations . . . would you want God
to DESTROY your country like he did biblical Egypt . . . for
opposing HIS DIVINE PLAN?

6. MALCOLM X AT YALE

Speaking, as always, in behalf of "The Honorable Elijah Muhammad," Malcolm X journeyed to Yale University in 1962 to debate with Herbert Wright, then National Youth Secretary of the NAACP.

The first third of this Yale Speech is Malcolm's attempt to put the Black Muslims' doctrine in world perspective. One may dispute, as Herbert Wright did, the lessons Malcolm draws from current history, but this lecture shows once again how the Black Muslims are struggling to give their doctrine the advantages of learning and information. Malcolm's point is that the world situation demands that the American Negro have a separate state and that even such threats as the Communist take-over in Cuba will not subside until that all-Negro state is brought into being.

This talk has a particularly scorching indictment of middle-class Negroes. Several people who were present at the debate have told me that Herbert Wright became difficult at times, for Malcolm, and that Malcolm responded with an unusual amount of bile. This was one of a series of debates between Wright and Malcolm X, and the NAACP finally ordered a halt to the encounters.

Remembering that the Black Muslims have a prohibition against voting, the reader will be particularly interested in Malcolm's arguments as to why the majority of American Negroes do not vote. He sees this apathy at the polls as a rebellion against "integration-minded" Negro leadership. And this may be a commentary on why the Muslims have themselves decided to enter politics.

IN BEHALF OF my beloved leader and teacher, The Honor-

able Elijah Muhammad, and the many young Muslims who follow him, we wish to thank you for this opportunity to explain our position today in what we feel to be the only solution to the serious race problems confronting America and the entire troubled Western World.

In this crucial hour in which we live today, it is essential that our minds constantly be kept open to reality. We have both races here in this Yale Law School Auditorium tonight. Let us not be emotional. Let us be governed and guided only by facts.

I represent Mr. Elijah Muhammad, the spiritual head of the fastest-growing group of Black Muslims in the Western Hemisphere. We who follow him know that he has been divinely taught and sent to us by God Himself. We believe that the miserable plight of the 20 million black people in America is the fulfillment of divine prophecy. We believe that the serious race problem that our presence here poses for America is also the fulfillment of divine prophecy. We also believe the presence today in America of The Honorable Elijah Muhammad, his teachings among the so-called Negroes, and his naked warning to America concerning her treatment of these so-called Negroes is all the fulfillment of divine prophecy.

Thus, when Mr. Muhammad declares that the only solution to America's race problem is complete separation of the two races, he is fulfilling that which was predicted by all of the biblical prophets to take place in this day. But, because Mr. Muhammad takes this uncompromising stand, those who don't understand biblical prophecy wrongly label him as a racist and as a hate teacher, or as being anti-white, or as teaching Black Supremacy. So tonight, while we are all here together, face to face, we can question and examine for ourselves the wisdom or the folly of what Mr. Muhammad is teaching.

Studying world conditions in the light of facts, facing reality as grown men and women . . . seeing things not as we would like them to be, but as they really are . . . only then can we determine the rightness, the validity, the divine origin of Mr. Muhammad and the solution which he offers as the only hope for America's 20 million so-called Negroes, and also as the only hope for this troubled Western World.

If Mr. Muhammad's solution is from God, is it in time to

save 20 million so-called Negroes? Is it in time to save America? Is it in time to save the Western World? Let us look closely and see.

The Western World finds itself today constantly engulfed in crisis after crisis. The ingredients for disaster lurk constantly on all sides . . . both at home and abroad. The Western World's leading diplomats are whispering in the halls of the UN that catastrophe can come any moment, any hour, any second.

Whether this grave crisis be studied at the international level, the national level, or the local level, we will discover the primary ingredient always encountered, in one form or another, is the race issue . . . the race question . . . the race problem. Whether it is the Congo, Algeria, South Africa, China, Cuba, or Panama.

Let us take the advice Paul gave in the bible; let us toss our emotions aside and reason together. Let us look closely at this chaotic world-picture before us, and in the light of the facts let us then determine if Mr. Muhammad's divine solution fits the picture before us.

But many of you may be asking yourselves: "Why should we listen to this little so-called Negro . . . this little Georgia-born ex-slave? What can he do? What can he tell us?

Well, my friends, the Western World's most learned diplomats have failed to solve this grave race problem. Her learned politicians have failed. Her learned theologians have failed. Her learned legal experts have failed. Her sociologists have failed. Her civil leaders have failed. Her fraternal leaders have even failed.

Since the Western World's most skillful scientists and scholars have failed to solve this race problem, it is time for us to sit down tonight and reason together, and I'm certain we will be forced to agree that it takes God Himself to solve this grave racial dilemma. When we face these facts, we see the necessity for DIVINE intervention . . . we see the necessity for a DIVINE SOLUTION.

If God is going to intervene, will He come Himself, or will He send someone with His solution? Will we be able to accept this divine solution when it comes? How will we know if the Messenger who brings us the solution is really a man from God? What yardstick will we use to measure him?

Will this man of God be someone from Harvard, Yale, Columbia, Howard, or Tuskegee? Will this man of God be a black man or a white man?

Will he be a theologian or preacher from one of the prevailing religions of the Western World? Will he be a politician from one of the major political parties? What type of man do you think God would choose to deliver His solution to this troubled Western World? How are we to determine whether or not Mr. Muhammad is a man from God? And, how are we to determine if it is time for God Himself to intervene?

Let us not be emotional; let us reason together. Look around us at the condition of the world. Never before has man had in his hands the power to destroy human life on such a vast scale. Never before has there been such propaganda, mass lies, mass suspicion, mass confusion, mass dissatisfaction, mass unrest, mass hatreds . . . and the ingredients for such mass bloodshed.

Never before has America made so many crucial blunders, one after another, and suffered such great loss of prestige in the eyes of the world, despite the advice of her expert advisors.

The U-2 spy plane incident caused the President of the strongest country on earth to be tricked, trapped and exposed before the whole world as a liar . . . despite the advice of expert advisors.

At the Paris Summit Conference, the same President was cursed, ridiculed, and humiliated again before the eyes of the entire world . . . despite the advice of his expert advisors.

In Korea, students, mere children, toppled the government of Syngman Rhee, the best friend America had in the Far East, despite the advice of her expert advisors.

In Turkey, children toppled the government of Menderes, America's best friend in the Middle East . . . despite the advice of expert advisors.

In Tokyo, students, mere children again, defied the President to come to Japan, and blocked him from entering after he had traveled thousands of miles from home and had arrived at their back door . . . a most humiliating insult . . . despite the advice of his expert advisors.

And Cuba, a little midget island-government in the Caribbean, is challenging Giant America, accusing her of eco-

nomic aggression, confiscating all of her investments, and getting unexpected support from Mexico and other strategically located Latin American countries . . . and all of this, despite the advice of her expert advisors.

My friends, if the expert politicians, the expert theologians, the expert diplomats and other scientists, professors and scholars have failed to devise a solution to these grave world problems, surely you will agree that it is now time for God to send us someone with a solution from Himself.

Is Mr. Muhammad from God? Is he on time? Does his divine solution fit the events of today?

Look at the racial volcano that has erupted in the Congo, with the ingredients present for an even greater racial explosion building up into what could easily touch off the dreaded 3rd World War . . . and once again the diplomats in the UN are whispering that Western Civilization is tottering on the brink of disaster.

Why are the Africans in the Congo rising against the white Belgian oppressors? Why are the Africans in Kenya rising against their white British oppressors? Why are the Africans in Angola rising against their white Portuguese oppressors? Why are the Africans in Algeria rising against their white French oppressors? In short: Why is the black man today all over Africa rising up against his white European overlords?

In the Congo, Central Africa, the black man is saying, "We must have our own land." In Kenya, East Africa, the black man is saying, "We must have our own land." In Angola, West Africa, the black man is saying, "We must have our own land." In Algeria, North Africa, the black man is saying, "We must have our own land." Even deep into South Africa, all over the entire African continent, the only solution in the minds of the awakening black man is: "We must have our own land."

The cry of the black man in Africa for the return of his own land is so widespread, so unrelenting, so uncompromising . . . it stands to reason that only God Himself is inspiring him and driving him onward in this spirit of freedom. If God has made the black man in Africa realize he cannot rest until he has some land of his own . . . surely that same God will look westward toward America and see

20 million black people here, SECOND-CLASS CITIZENS, who are also in dire need of some land that we can call our own.

If Mr. Muhammad says "some land of our own" is God's solution to this grave race problem, why land? Why is land so important to everyone today?

The white man in Great Britain could once boast that his control extended over so much of the black man's land that the sun never set on the British Empire. Today, when the sun rises, we can hardly find the British Empire.

How important is land? Well, look what happened to the British Empire when she lost the lands she had colonized in Asia: lands like India, China, Burma, Malaya, etc. . . . her inability to continue robbing Asia of the natural resources produced by the land almost wrecked the British economy, decreased her military strength and her political prestige so low she could no longer use "force" to hold her African colonies.

As her grip on the black man's land loosened, Britain dwindled. Loss of land meant loss of Empire . . . loss of wealth, power, and of prestige.

As the black men in Africa and Asia regain control over their lands, the French, Belgians, Dutch, Portuguese, Spanish, and all other European Empires also begin to crumble and topple downward . . .

As we face these facts, we are forced to agree that the economy of white Europe, the military power of white Europe, and the political prestige of white Europe was based upon the lands in Africa and Asia which they had taken from the BLACK MAN.

The combined powers of white Europe have not been able to stem this black tide in Africa that is sweeping aside the shackles of colonial slavery. The Africans have become militant and are marching toward freedom. Africa is the only continent where a new nation is being born every day . . . and these new nations are taking their seats in the family of other independent nations symbolized by the United Nations.

And, this fast-growing black block formed by these newly born African nations, united with our Darker Brothers in Asia, can already easily out-vote the white colonial powers in the UN who had formerly enslaved them. These

newly born independent black nations can also take a firm stand in behalf of other black people all over the world who are still enslaved, persecuted, exploited . . . or deprived of their basic rights.

As the rise of these newly independent black nations collapses the economic, military, and political strength of America's allies in white Europe, what effect does this have upon white America?

Does white America face the same black web in which the colonial powers of white Europe find themselves entangled? And, if so, how will this affect America's attitude toward the black people of Africa? How will this affect America's attitude toward the 20 million black people who are yet suffering the bondage of so-called second-class citizenship right here in America . . . 20 million so-called Negroes who have also been deprived of freedom, justice, and equality . . . 20 million so-called Negroes who not only have been deprived of their civil rights, but who have even been deprived of their HUMAN RIGHTS . . . the right to hold their heads up, and to live in dignity like other human beings.

Let us not be emotional, but let us face these facts. Let us reason together. This has become a serious problem for America, and for the entire world.

Will the Divine Solution that God has given Mr. Elijah Muhammad help white America avert the racial dilemma in which the awakening dark nations of Africa and Asia have already placed America's allies in white Europe?

Before we can intelligently decide to accept or reject Mr. Muhammad's solution, let us take a closer look at America itself:

America is the richest and most powerful nation on this earth. Her President is almost like a "god," for he has in his hands almost every other country on this earth. Therefore, every four years, when a new President, or "god," is about to be selected, the eyes of even the foreign nations are turned toward the American elections . . . for they too are wondering who, what type of man, will be the next "god."

Yet, at the two great political conventions in which the two candidates are selected, despite America's need to impress, and favorably influence the foreign nations, foreign

policy is never the great controversial issue . . . the controversial issue is always over domestic policy . . . the CIVIL RIGHTS ISSUE . . . in which the so-called American Negro is the primary figure . . . the STAR on the world stage . . . for it is he who holds the balance of power in all elections . . . it is he who can easily determine "who" will be the next "god."

Therefore, this great political drama not only stars the Negro, but all the political schemes are designed primarily to woo him, to please him, to tempt him, ensnare him, to get his allegiance and capitalize upon his political support.

The Negro's position is most strategic, but his mental condition is too pathetic for him to take intelligent advantage of this vital position "fate" has placed him in. The American Negro is suffering from a mental sickness. His mind has been "tampered" with by his slave master.

The Western World is sick. America is sick . . . but the Negro in America is the sickest of them all. The sickening condition of the Negro in America is infecting Uncle Sam's entire body and endangering the security and future of the whole Western World.

Mr. Muhammad says that only after the American Negro's condition is "corrected" will Uncle Sam's health improve . . . for only then will Uncle Sam look "healthy" in the inquiring eyes of the fast-awakening dark world.

Since we see the vital necessity of correcting the miserable condition of the American Negro, and we must also agree that all other efforts to solve this problem have failed, will Mr. Muhammad's "prescription" cure the ailments of these 20 million second-class citizens?

Many of you will say: "No! Muhammad is a Black Supremist. He is an extremist. He stresses race too much. He is a racist."

My friends: If you were to see a man attired in white, with a sharp instrument in his hands, bending over someone who is prostrate on a table, your lack of understanding might compel you to shout, "murderer!"

But when you know the place is a hospital, the sleeping man is a patient, the man attired in white is a surgeon, and the sharp instrument must be used to perform some surgery that is necessary to save the patient's life . . . you

can then accept the fact that although the operation is very painful, it must be performed.

Uncle Sam is sick, because he has a black "lump" growing in his white body that doesn't belong there, and this black "growth" is getting larger every day, and increasing Uncle Sam's internal pains. God himself has ordained that this surgery must be performed, for if the 20 million rapidly increasing so-called Negroes are not separated from the white parts of the body, it will soon cause the death and destruction of Uncle Sam.

God has given Mr. Muhammad some sharp truth. It is like a two-edged sword. It cuts into you. It causes you great pain, but if you can take it, it will cure you and save you from what otherwise would be CERTAIN DEATH.

In your mental anguish many of you will emotionally insist that Mr. Muhammad is not teaching the real religion of Islam. You will still insist that he is teaching a racial, economic, and political philosophy.

My friends, Islam is the religion taught by all of the prophets: Noah, Lot, Abraham, Moses, and even Jesus. Islam is the true name of the religion God gave to the prophets in the past to cure their people of whatever moral or spiritual ailments that were afflicting them in that day.

Since we have examined the ailments of the crumbling Western World, and the ills that are infecting America . . . let us look more closely at the miserable condition of the American Negro:

Here are 20 million people who have lost their original identity; they cannot even speak their own mother tongue. How can 20 million people lose their language? What happened to it? What was it? Why don't they at least know what it was?

Why don't the educated Negroes know something about their own history, their own culture, the last names of their forefathers, their own nationality, their own country, their own flag, their own religion, and their own God?

My friends, surely you will agree that no other people in history, biblical or otherwise, have been so completely stripped and robbed by their slave master of all knowledge concerning their own kind . . . and because of this, no other

people in history, biblical or otherwise, have ever presented such a problem to their former slave masters or to the world . . . as the problem created by the presence of the 20 million so-called Negroes here in America today.

The New York *Tribune,* in an editorial (Feb. 5, 1960), pointed out that out of 11 million qualified Negro voters, only 2,700,000 actually took time to vote. This means that, roughly speaking, only 3 million of the 11 million Negroes who are qualified to vote take an active part . . . and the remaining 8 million remain voluntarily inactive, and yet it is this small minority of Negro voters who help determine who will be the next President.

If who will be the next President can be influenced by 3 million Negro voters, it is easy to see why the presidential candidates of both political parties put on such a false show with the civil rights bill, and with promises of integration. They must woo or impress the 3 million voting Negroes who are the actual "integration seekers."

If so much fuss is made over these 3 million "integration seekers," what would the presidential candidates have to do to appease the 8 million non-voting Negroes if they ever decided to become politically active in this election year?

Who are the 8 million non-voting Negroes, what do they want, and why don't they vote?

The 3 million voters are the so-called middle- (or high-) class Negroes, referred to by Howard University Sociology Professor E. Franklin Frazier, as the "BLACK BOURGEOISIE," who have been educated to think as patriotic individualists, with no racial pride . . . who believe in, and look forward to, the future "integrated-intermarried" society promised them by the Negro politicians . . . and therefore, this "integration-minded" 3 million remain an active part of the white-controlled political parties. But it must never be overlooked, that these 3 million integration seekers are only a small minority of the 11 million qualified voters.

The 8 million non-voting Negroes are the majority, the downtrodden black masses. They have refused to vote, or to take part in politics, because they reject the Uncle Tom approach of the "clergy-politician" leadership that has been

hand-picked for the American Negroes by the white man himself.

The clergy-politician leadership does not speak for the Negro majority; they don't speak for the black masses. They speak for the "BLACK BOURGEOISIE," the "brain-washed" (white-minded) middle-class minority . . . who, because they are ashamed of black, and don't want to be identified with black or as being black, are seeking to lose this "identity" by mingling, mixing, intermarrying, and in-tegration with the white man.

The race problem cannot be solved by listening to this white-minded (brainwashed) minority. The white man must try to learn what does the majority want. The next President would be wise to try and learn what the black masses want. And, the only way to find this out is by listening to the man who speaks for the black masses of America.

I declare to you and to the entire world, that the man here in America who speaks for the majority, the down-trodden, dissatisfied black masses . . . is this same man whom so many thousands of our people are flocking toward to see and hear . . . this same Mr. Muhammad who is labeled by you as a Black Supremist, and as a Racist!

If the 3 million middle-class Negroes are casting their ballots for integration and intermarriage . . . what do the non-voting black masses who are in the minority want? Find out what the black masses want, and then perhaps America's grave race problem can be solved.

The black masses are tired of following these hand-picked Negro "leaders" who sound like professional beggars, as they cry year after year for white America to accept us as first-class citizens.

Since this clergy-politician "leadership," which was care-fully hand-picked for us by the white man, has failed to solve the problem for the downtrodden black masses . . . God Himself has stepped into the picture, and has made Messenger Elijah Muhammad a wise, fearless, and uncom-promising spokesman for the 20 million black people here in America, who, behind the Divine Leadership of this man of God, will now never be satisfied until we have a home in a land that we can proudly call our own.

We have accepted your invitation to come here to Yale

University Law School this evening to let you know first hand why 20 million so-called Negroes cannot integrate with white America . . . why white America, after 100 years of religious hypocrisy and political trickery will never accept us as first-class citizens here . . . and why we must therefore seek some separate territory of our own.

In your blind emotion, again many of you will cry out that this is wrong, that this is not religion, that this is not Islam . . . that this is just another economic-political philosophy.

I must remind you to keep an open mind. Let your own Christian bible be the judge:

You credit Moses with being a religious man, a man of God, doing God's work. Yet, what did Moses actually do? What did Moses teach? Moses freed his people from their slave master. Moses told the oppressor of his people: "Let my people go." Moses separated his people from their masters, and then led them into a separate territory of their own.

You admit Moses was a man of God, yet you will have to agree Moses did not teach integration. Moses taught separation. Moses didn't take time to dwell on religious practices. He just let his people know that he represented the God of their forefathers, whose desire it was for them to be separated from their slave master and placed in a land that they could call their own. Mr. Muhammad's message and mission today is the same as that of the biblical Moses. Mr. Muhammad is a modern Moses in this modern-day house of bondage.

Many of you will cry out that you don't go by what Moses said or did, but rather by what Jesus said. You claim that Jesus taught love and that Mr. Muhammad teaches hate.

But, my friends, have you really read the bible? Are you familiar with Luke 14:26 where Jesus taught: "If any man come to me, and hate not his father, and mother, and wife, and children, and brethren, and sisters, yes, and even his own life also, he cannot be my disciple."

In other words, Jesus taught that you must hate everyone in your family, even your own self . . . and Muhammad

teaches us to love our brothers and sisters . . . yet you say Muhammad teaches hate and that Jesus taught love.

Many of you will say that Jesus was no respecter of persons, that he came to all the world. You say Muhammad bars white people, therefore he can't be from God.

My friends, Jesus told his followers to go not the way of the Gentiles, go only to the "lost sheep." He definitely advised his followers to discriminate and make a distinction between the Gentiles and the "lost sheep."

But you still cry out that Jesus is coming back at the end of the world to make us all the same, make us one people . . . integrate us.

No, my friends, Jesus himself did not even advocate integration. He referred to the end of this world as that great "HARVEST TIME." He likened the people of today as "wheat and tares," who would be allowed to "grow together," or integrated, until God comes at the end of this world and separates the people Himself . . . then He would cause one to be burned in a Lake of Fire, and those whom He chooses for Himself He would save.

Jesus also spoke of the people of today as being like "sheep and goats," whom God would separate at the end of the world . . . some for salvation and some for destruction.

Jesus did not advocate integration; he advocated SEPARATION!

Noah's solution was not integration; in his day it was also a message of separation. Lot's solution was separation. And, remember, my friends, Jesus warned that "as it was in the days of Noah and Lot, so shall it be these last days" . . . not integration, but complete separation of the two races . . . or DESTRUCTION!

Surely you can now see that Mr. Muhammad's message, or solution, is the same as that of Noah, Lot, Moses, and Jesus. How can you still doubt if Mr. Muhammad is from God? What you really should be concerned about is has Mr. Muhammad come in time to save you; and what must you do now to save yourselves.

When Mr. Muhammad says that we must have some of these states, before you flinch and hold up your hands in "mock shock," let us look and see if 20 million so-called Negroes deserve such a solution.

If I were to collect the combined wages of everyone in this Yale University Law School auditorium tonight for just one week, I would have plenty of money. If I could work all of you for nothing for just one year I would be extremely rich. Well, what about the millions of black people who worked here in America as your slaves for over 300 years without one payday? What happened to their wages? Who collected the profits, or amassed the fortunes received from their free labor? Facing these unpleasant facts, surely you can easily see now how America became so rich so fast.

How will 20 million so-called Negroes today receive a "just compensation"? We have hundreds of years' "back pay" that is long overdue, and must be paid sooner or later . . . or is there to be no such thing as JUSTICE for your faithful ex-slaves?

The American government has appropriated billions of dollars to pay the Indians for lands taken from their foreparents by your foreparents.

Again I say, my friends, let us reason together: surely you will agree that God is more just than your government . . . yet your government has felt morally and legally obligated to pay billions of dollars to the Indians for the crime committed against them.

What about the 20 million so-called Negroes! If the Indians must be paid for land taken from them, what about the free labor and lives of our foreparents that were taken from us for over 300 years?

If the white politicians have agreed that the Indians should be paid for their lands . . . what price of payment will the GOD OF JUSTICE demand for 20 million black people who were robbed of our labor, lives, identity, culture, history . . . and even our human dignity?

What will God's price be? What will God's solution be? Can America pay God's price? And, if not, what will be the alternative?

The handwriting is on the wall for America. As America faces crisis after crisis . . . as America sees dangerous troubles mounting on all sides . . . and as America stares with stubborn blindness, refusing to read the handwriting on the wall . . . since her "experts" have shown they are unable to read its meaning, will America now accept an

ambassador from God, a Divine Messenger, a Warner, to read the handwriting for her and tell her what solution she must accept . . . ?

Or, will America blindly reject God's Messenger, and in so doing bring on her own Divine Destruction? I trust you will weigh well these words.

A SUMMING UP:
LOUIS LOMAX INTERVIEWS
MALCOLM X

LOMAX: Minister Malcolm, we are all by now familiar with your basic philosophy; we have heard you speak, seen you on television, and read your remarks in magazines and newspapers. By now, I think, everybody knows your position that the white man is a devil, a man incapable of doing right; you hold that the black man is of God's divine nature, that he fell from power because of weakness; you hold further that the white man's rule over the earth was scheduled to end in 1914, but that his end has been delayed because of the need to get the American Negro into the fold of black brotherhood.

MALCOLM X: Yes, sir, that is what The Honorable Elijah Muhammad teaches us. The white devil's time is up; it has been up for almost fifty years now. It has taken us that long to get the deaf, dumb, and blind black men in the wilderness of North America to wake up and understand who they are. You see, sir, when a man understands who he is, who God is, who the devil is . . . then he can pick himself up out of the gutter; he can clean himself up and stand up like a man should before his God. This is why we teach that in order for a man to really understand himself he must be part of a nation; he must have some land of his own, a God of his own, a language of his own. Most of all he must have love and devotion for his own kind.

LOMAX: Wouldn't you say the Negro has a nation—America?

MALCOLM X: Sir, how can a Negro say America is *his* nation? He was brought here in chains; he was put in slavery and worked like a mule for three hundred years; he was separated from his land, his culture, his God, his language!

169

The Negro was taught to speak the white man's tongue, worship the white God, and accept the white man as his superior.

This is a white man's country, and the Negro is nothing but an ex-slave who is now trying to get himself integrated into the slave master's house.

And the slave master doesn't want you! You fought and bled and died in every war the white man waged, and he still won't give you justice. You nursed his baby and cleaned behind his wife, and he still won't give you freedom; you turned the other cheek while he lynched you and raped your women, but he still won't give you equality. Now, you integration-minded Negroes are trying to force yourselves on your former slave master, trying to make him accept you in his drawing room; you want to hang out with his women rather than with women of your own kind.

LOMAX: Are you suggesting that all of us who fight for integration are after a white woman?

MALCOLM X: I wouldn't say *all* of you, but let the evidence speak for itself. Check up on these integration leaders, and you will find that most of them are either married to or hooked up with some white woman. Take that meeting between James Baldwin and Robert Kennedy; practically everybody there was interracially married. Harry Belafonte is married to a white woman; Lorraine Hansberry is married to a white man; Lena Horne is married to a white man.

Now how can any Negro, man or woman, who sleeps with a white person speak for me? No black person married to a white person can speak for me!

LOMAX: Why?

MALCOLM X: Why? Because only a man who is ashamed of what he is will marry out of his race. There has to be something wrong when a man or a woman leaves his own people and marries somebody of another kind. Men who are proud of being black marry black women; women who are proud of being black marry black men.

This is particularly true when you realize that these Negroes who go for integration and intermarriage are linking up with the very people who lynched their fathers, raped their mothers, and put their kid sisters in the kitchen to scrub floors. Why would any black man in his right

mind want to marry a lyncher, a murderer, a rapist, a dope peddler, a gambler, a hog eater . . . Why would any black man want to marry a *devil* . . . for that's just what the white man is.

LOMAX: I have heard you say that a thousand times, but it always jolts me. Why do you call the white man a devil?

MALCOLM X: Because that's what he is. What do you want me to call him, a saint? Anybody who rapes, and plunders, and enslaves, and steals, and drops hell bombs on people . . . anybody who does these things is nothing but a devil.

Look, Lomax, history rewards all research. And history fails to record one single instance in which the white man —as a people—did good. They have always been devils; they always will be devils, and they are about to be destroyed. The final proof that they are devils lies in the fact that they are about to destroy themselves. Only a devil—and a stupid devil at that—would destroy himself!

Now why would I want to integrate with somebody marked for destruction?

The Honorable Elijah Muhammad teaches us to get away from the devil as soon and as fast as we can. This is why we are demanding a separate state. Tell the slave master we will no longer beg for crumbs from his table; let him give us some land of our own so we can go for ourselves. If he doesn't give us some land, there is going to be hell to pay. As I said at Howard University and Queens College, once the white man let the Negro get an education, the Negro began to want what the white man has. But he let Negroes get education and now they are demanding integration; they want to have exactly what he has. And the white man is not going to give it to them!

LOMAX: But we have made some gains. . . .

MALCOLM X: What gains? All you have gotten is tokenism —one or two Negroes in a job or at a lunch counter so the rest of you will be quiet. It took the United States Army to get one Negro in the University of Mississippi; it took troops to get a few Negroes in white schools at Little Rock and another dozen places in the South. It has been nine years since the Supreme Court decision outlawing segregated schools, yet less than ten per cent of the Negro students in the South are in integrated schools. That isn't integration, that's tokenism! In spite of all the dogs, and

fire hoses, and club-swinging policemen, I have yet to read of anybody eating an integrated hamburger in Birmingham.

You Negroes are not willing to admit it yet, but integration will not work. Why, it is against the white man's nature to integrate you into his house. Even if he wanted to, he could no more do it than a Model T can sprout wings and fly. It isn't in him.

Now The Honorable Elijah Muhammad says it would be the easiest thing in the world for the white man to destroy the Black Muslims. We contend that the white man is a devil. If he is not a devil, let him prove it!

He can't do it, Lomax; it isn't in him; it is against his nature.

He'll keep on granting tokenism; a few big Negroes will get big jobs, but the black masses will catch hell as long as they stay in the white man's house.

The only possible way out for the white man is to give us some land of our own; let us get out, get away from his wicked reign and go for ourselves.

But the white man will not do that, either. He is going to keep you integration-minded Negroes cooped up here in this country, and when you discover that the white man is a trickster, a devil, that he has no intentions of integrating, then you Negroes will run wild. That will be the time . . .

LOMAX: The time for what?

MALCOLM X: Only The Honorable Elijah Muhammad can answer that!

LOMAX: This is strong gospel, Minister Malcolm; many people, Negro and white, say what you preach amounts to hate, that your theology is actually anti-Semitic. What is your comment to that?

MALCOLM X: The white people who are guilty of white supremacy are trying to hide their own guilt by accusing The Honorable Elijah Muhammad of teaching black supremacy when he tries to uplift the mentality, the social, mental, and economic condition of the black people in this country. Jews who have been guilty of exploiting the black people in this country, economically, civically, and otherwise, hide behind—hide their guilt by accusing The Honorable Elijah Muhammad of being anti-Semitic, simply because he teaches our people to go into business for our-

selves and try and take over the economic leadership in our own community.

And since the white people collectively have practiced the worst form of hatred against Negroes in this country and they know that they are guilty of it, now when The Honorable Elijah Muhammad comes along and begins to list the historic deed—the historic attitude, the historic behavior of the white man in this country toward the black people in this country, again, the white people are so guilty, and they can't stop doing these things to make Mr. Muhammad appear wrong, so they hide their wrong by saying "he is teaching hatred." History is not hatred. Actually we are Muslims because we believe in the religion of Islam. We believe in one God. We believe in Muhammad as the Apostle of God. We practice the principles of the religion of Islam, which mean prayer, charity, fasting, brotherhood, and The Honorable Elijah Muhammad teaches us that since the Western society is deteriorating, it has become overrun with immorality, that God is going to judge it and destroy it, and the only way the black people who are in this society can be saved is not to integrate into this corrupt society but separate ourselves from it, reform ourselves, lift up our moral standards and try and be godly—try to integrate with God—instead of trying to integrate with the white man, or try and imitate God instead of trying to imitate the white man.

LOMAX: It is suggested also that your movement preaches violence.

MALCOLM X: No, sir. The black people of this country have been victims of violence at the hands of the white men for four hundred years, and following the ignorant Negro preachers, we have thought that it was godlike to turn the other cheek to the brute that was brutalizing us. Today The Honorable Elijah Muhammad is showing black people in this country that, just as the white man and every other person on this earth has God-given rights, natural rights, civil rights, any kind of rights that you can think of, when it comes to defending himself, black people—we should have the right to defend ourselves also. And, because The Honorable Elijah Muhammad makes black people brave enough, men enough to defend ourselves no matter what the odds are, the white man runs around here

with a doctrine that Mr. Muhammad is advocating violence when he is actually telling Negroes to defend themselves against violent people.

LOMAX: Reverend Martin Luther King teaches a doctrine of nonviolence. What is your attitude toward this philosophy?

MALCOLM X: The white man supports Reverend Martin Luther King, subsidizes Reverend Martin Luther King, so that Reverend Martin Luther King can continue to teach the Negroes to be defenseless—that's what you mean by nonviolent—be defenseless in the face of one of the most cruel beasts that has ever taken people into captivity— that's this American white man, and they have proved it throughout the country by the police dogs and the police clubs. A hundred years ago they used to put on a white sheet and use a bloodhound against Negroes. Today they have taken off the white sheet and put on police uniforms and traded in the bloodhounds for police dogs, and they're still doing the same thing. Just as Uncle Tom, back during slavery, used to keep the Negroes from resisting the blood-hound or resisting the Ku Klux Klan by teaching them to love their enemies or pray for those who use them despite-fully, today Martin Luther King is just a twentieth-century or modern Uncle Tom or religious Uncle Tom, who is doing the same thing today to keep Negroes defenseless in the face of attack that Uncle Tom did on the plantation to keep *those* Negroes defenseless in the face of the attack of the Klan in that day.

Now, the goal of Dr. Martin Luther King is to give Negroes a chance to sit in a segregated restaurant beside the same white man who has brutalized them for four hundred years. The goal of Martin Luther King is to get Negroes to forgive the people, the people who have brutal-ized them for four hundred years, by lulling them to sleep and making them forget what those whites have done to them, but the masses of black people today don't go for what Martin Luther King is putting down.

LOMAX: Minister Malcolm, you often speak of unity among our people. Unity for what?

MALCOLM X: The Honorable Elijah Muhammad teaches us that God now is about to establish a kingdom on this earth based upon brotherhood and peace, and the white man is against brotherhood and the white man is against peace.

His history on this earth has proved that. Nowhere in history has he been brotherly toward anyone. The only time he is brotherly toward you is when he can use you, when he can exploit you, when he will oppress you, when you will submit to him, and since his own history makes him unqualified to be an inhabitant or a citizen in the kingdom of brotherhood, The Honorable Elijah Muhammad teaches us that God is about to eliminate that particular race from this earth. Since they are due for elimination, we don't want to be with them. We are not trying to integrate with that which we know has come to the end of its rope. We are trying to separate from it and get with something that is more lasting, and we think that God is more lasting than the white man.

LOMAX: Then your movement does not share the integration goals of the NAACP, CORE, Martin Luther King's movement, and the Student Nonviolent movement.

MALCOLM X: You don't integrate with a sinking ship. You don't do anything to further your stay aboard a ship that you see is going to go down to the bottom of the ocean. Moses tried to separate his people from Pharaoh, and when he tried, the magicians tried to fool the people into staying with Pharaoh, and we look upon these other organizations that are trying to get Negroes to integrate with this doomed white man as nothing but modern-day magicians, and The Honorable Elijah Muhammad is a modern-day Moses trying to separate us from the modern-day Pharaoh. Until the white man in America sits down and talks with The Honorable Elijah Muhammad, he won't even know what the race problem—what makes the race problem what it is. Just like Pharaoh couldn't get a solution to his problem until he talked to Moses, or Nebuchadnezzar or Belshazzar couldn't get a solution to his problem until he talked to Daniel, the white man in America today will never understand the race problem or come anywhere near getting a solution to the race problem until he talks to The Honorable Elijah Muhammad. Mr. Muhammad will give him God's analysis, not some kind of political analysis or psychologist's analysis, or some kind of clergyman's analysis, but God's anaylsis. That's the analysis that Moses gave Pharaoh; that's the analysis that Daniel gave Belshazzar. Today we have a

modern Belshazzar and a modern Pharaoh sitting in Washington, D. C.

LOMAX: I am struck by the fact that each of the biblical figures you mentioned—Pharaoh, Nebuchadnezzar, and Belshazzar—came to a rather sorry end. Are you willing to complete the analogy and say the American white establishment will come to a bitter end, perhaps be destroyed?

MALCOLM X: I have spoken on this many times, and I am sure you know what The Honorable Elijah Muhammad teaches on this. But since we are on record I will—as they sometimes say in Harlem—make it plain.

Now, sir, God is going to punish this wicked devil for his misdeeds toward black people. Just as plagues were visited on Pharaoh so will pestilences and disasters be visited on the white man. Why, it has already started: God has begun to send them heat when they expect cold; he sends them cold when they expect heat. Their crops are dying, their children are being born with all kinds of deformities, the rivers and the lakes are coming out of the belly of the earth to wash them away.

Not only that, but God has started slapping their planes down from the sky. Last year [1962] God brought down one of their planes loaded with crackers whose fathers had lynched your and my brothers and sisters. They were from your state, Lomax, down there in Georgia where both you and Mr. Muhammad come from. Now, long before that plane crash I predicted [in Los Angeles] that God was going to strike back at the devil for the way white cops brutalized our brothers in Los Angeles. When the plane fell, I said this was God's way of letting his wrath be known. I said much the same thing when that submarine— the *Thresher*—went down to the bottom of the sea. Now for this I was called names—some of these Uncle Tom Negroes rushed into print to condemn me for what I had said. But what was wrong with what I said? Everybody has a God and believes that his God will deliver him and protect him from his enemies! Why can't the black man have a God? What's so wrong when a black man says his God will protect him from his white foe? If Jehovah can slay Philistines for the Jews, why can't Allah slay crackers for the so-called Negro?

LOMAX: Is that the reasoning behind your remark after the assassination of President Kennedy? You are reported to have

said that Kennedy's death was an instance of "chickens coming home to roost."

MALCOLM X: Yes, but let's clear up what I said. I did not say that Kennedy's death was a reason for rejoicing. That is not what I meant at all. Rather, I meant that the death of Kennedy was the result of a long line of violent acts, the culmination of hate and suspicion and doubt in this country. You see, Lomax, this country has allowed white people to kill and brutalize those they don't like. The assassination of Kennedy is a result of that way of life and thinking. The chickens came home to roost; that's all there is to it. America—at the death of the President—just reaped what it had been sowing.

LOMAX: But you were disciplined for making these remarks; The Honorable Elijah Muhammad has publicly rebuked you and has ordered you not to speak in public until further notice.

MALCOLM X: This is true. I was wrong; The Messenger had warned me not to say anything about the death of the President, and I omitted any reference to that tragedy in my main speech. But during a question-and-answer period someone asked about the meaning of the Kennedy assassination, and I said it was a case of chickens coming home to roost. Now about that suspension—it's just as if you have cut off a radio. The radio is still there, but it makes no sound. You can cut it back on when it pleases you.

LOMAX: How long do you think this suspension will last?

MALCOLM X: Only the Honorable Elijah Muhammad can answer that. I don't think it will be permanent.

LOMAX: Then you do expect to return to your duties?

MALCOLM X: Yes, sir.

LOMAX: And you will continue to preach separation from the white man?

MALCOLM X: Yes, sir.

LOMAX: Just a moment, if I may, Minister Malcolm. Now, you talk about separation from the white man.

MALCOLM X: Yes, sir.

LOMAX: You even take it so far as to suggest that we shouldn't even get on airplanes and ships with white people. Am I correct in that?

MALCOLM X: Yes, sir, on the whole. Yes.

LOMAX: But Minister Malcolm, few people, Negro or white, travel as much as you and I do. You spend much of your life getting on and off aircraft. Don't you fear that you just

might be aboard when God sees fit to slap down a jet and
kill a few score white people?

MALCOLM X: Sir, my faith in God is such that I am not
afraid. I know that I will not die until my time comes. But
if I am aboard one of these vessels, I will be happy to give
my life to see some of these white devils die. Like Samson,
I am ready to pull down the white man's temple, knowing
full well that I will be destroyed by the falling rubble.

LOMAX: But Minister Malcolm, you make no accommodation for the changes that have come about as a result of
the Negro Revolt. What do you think will be the results
of the current demonstrations against segregation?

MALCOLM X: Lomax, as you know, these Negro leaders have
been telling the white man everything is all right, everything is under control, and they have been telling the white
man that Mr. Muhammad is wrong, don't listen to him.
But everything that Mr. Muhammad has been saying is
going to come to pass, is now coming to pass. Now the
Negro leaders are standing up saying that we are about to
have a racial explosion. You're going to have a racial explosion, and a racial explosion is more dangerous than an
atomic explosion. It's going to explode because black people are dissatisfied; they're dissatisfied not only with the
white man, but they're dissatisfied with these Negroes who
have been sitting around here posing as leaders and spokesmen for black people and actually making the problem
worse instead of making the problem better.

LOMAX: Do you deny that Negroes are now getting the
protection of the Federal Government; after all, both the
President and the Attorney General have come to our aid.

MALCOLM X: You never will get protection from the Federal Government. Just like King is asking Kennedy to go to
Alabama to stand in a doorway—to put his body in a doorway. That's like asking the fox to protect you from the
wolf! The masses of black people can see this, and it is
only the Negro leadership, the bourgeois, hand-picked, handful of Negroes who think that they're going to get some
kind of respect, recognition, or protection from the Government. The Government is responsible for what is happen-
ing to black people in this country. The President has power.
You notice he didn't send any troops into Birmingham to
protect the Negroes when the dogs were biting the Negroes.
The only time he sent troops into Birmingham was when

the Negroes erupted, and then the President sent the troops in there, not to protect the Negroes, but to protect them white people down there from those erupting Negroes.

LOMAX: Are not Negroes American citizens?

MALCOLM X: If they were citizens, you wouldn't have a race problem. If the Emancipation Proclamation was authentic, you wouldn't have a race problem. If the 13th, 14th and 15th Amendments to the Constitution were authentic, you wouldn't have a race problem. If the Supreme Court desegregation decision was authentic, you wouldn't have a race problem. All of this is hypocrisy that has been practiced by the so-called white so-called liberal for the past four hundred years that compounds the problem, makes it more complicated, instead of eliminating the problem.

LOMAX: What, then, do you see as the final result of all these demonstrations?

MALCOLM X: Any time you put too many sparks around a powder keg, the thing is going to explode, and if the thing that explodes is still inside the house, then the house will be destroyed. So The Honorable Elijah Muhammad is telling the white man, "Get this powder keg out of your house—let the black people in this country separate from you, while there's still time." If the black man is allowed to separate and go into some land of his own where he can solve his own problems, there won't be any explosion, and the Negroes who want to stay with the white man, let them stay with the white man—but those who want to leave, let them go with The Honorable Elijah Muhammad.

LOMAX: Now that you have mentioned The Messenger, I would like to ask you about this article in the [New York] *Amsterdam News*. . . .

MALCOLM X: It's a lie. Any article that says there is a "minor" difference between Mr. Muhammad and me is a lie. How could there be any difference between The Messenger and me? I am his slave, his servant, his son. He is the leader, the only spokesman for the Black Muslims.

But I will tell you this: The Messenger has seen God. He was with Allah and was given divine patience with the devil. He is willing to wait for Allah to deal with this devil. Well, sir, the rest of us Black Muslims have not seen God, we don't have this gift of divine patience with the devil. The younger Black Muslims want to see some action.

LOMAX: What kind of action?

MALCOLM X: Some things are better done than said.

LOMAX: According to your own newspaper, one of the things you Muslims may *do* in the near future is vote.

MALCOLM X: Yes. After long and prayerful consideration, The Honorable Elijah Muhammad allowed us to announce the possibility of Muslims voting. The announcement came at our annual Saviour's Day convention in Chicago.

LOMAX: What does it mean?

MALCOLM X: Mr. Muhammad is the only one who can explain that fully. However, I can say that we may register and be ready to vote. Then we will seek out candidates who represent our interests and support them. They need not be Muslims; what we want are race men who will speak out for our people.

LOMAX: There are rumors that you may run against Adam Clayton Powell.

MALCOLM X: Why must I run against a Negro? We have had enough of Negroes running against and fighting each other. The better bet is that we would put a Muslim candidate in the field against a devil, somebody who is against all we stand for.

LOMAX: What are the chances of the Black Muslims joining us in picket lines for better jobs? . . .

MALCOLM X: As I told you, only Mr. Muhammad can answer that. But let me tell you something: Better jobs and housing are only temporary solutions. They are aspects of tokenism and don't go to the heart of the problem.

This is why integration will not work. It assumes that the two races, black and white, are equal and can be made to live as one. This is not true.

The white man is by nature a devil and must be destroyed. The black man will inherit the earth; he will resume control, taking back the position he held centuries ago when the white devil was crawling around the caves of Europe on his all fours. Before the white devil came into our lives we had a civilization, we had a culture, we were living in silks and satins. Then he put us in chains and placed us aboard the "Good Ship Jesus," and we have lived in hell ever since.

Now the white man's time is over. Tokenism will not help him, and it will doom us. Complete separation will save us—and who knows, it might make God decide to give the white devil a few more years.

SUGGESTED ADDITIONAL READING

Baldwin, James. *The Fire Next Time.* New York: Dial Press, 1963.

Bennett, Lerone, Jr. *Before the Mayflower.* Chicago: Johnson Publishing Co., 1962.

Beynon, Erdmann D. "The Voodoo Cult Among Negro Migrants in Detroit," *The American Journal of Sociology,* XLIII, No. 6 (May 1938).

Franklin, John Hope. *From Slavery to Freedom.* New York: Alfred A. Knopf, 1956.

Frazier, E. Franklin. *Black Bourgeoisie.* Chicago: The Free Press of Glencoe, 1957.

Handlin, Oscar. *Race and Nationality in American Life.* Boston: Little, Brown, 1957.

Herskovits, Melville J. *Myth of the Negro Past.* New York: Harper & Brothers, 1941.

Leibrecht, Walter, and others. *Religion and Culture: Essays in Honor of Paul Tillich.* New York: Harper & Brothers, 1959.

Lincoln, C. Eric. *The Black Muslims in America.* Boston: Beacon Press, 1962.

Lomax, Louis E. *The Reluctant African.* New York: Harper & Brothers, 1960.

————*The Negro Revolt.* New York: Harper & Brothers, 1962.

Myrdal, Gunnar. *An American Dilemma.* New York: Harper & Brothers, 1944.

INDEX

Abyssinian Baptist Church
 (New York), 39
Africa
 Akbar brings promise of help
  from, 86–87
 culture of
  matrilineal society, 32
  political institutions, 32
  religion, 33–34
 knowledge of history of, 59
 languages of, 32–33
 Malcolm X in, 62, 130
 nationalism in, 157–158
African Methodist Episcopal
 Church, 38
African Methodist Episcopal
 Zion Church, 39
Airplane crash (1962), 176
Al-Azhar University
 Akbar Muhammad at, 84
 Elijah Muhammad at, 122
Alcohol, Malcolm X and, 51
Ali, John X, 72, 86, 90
 administrative ability of, 81,
  82
Allah
 as black, 22, 55, 140
 divine plagues of, 124
 Elijah Muhammad as Mes-
  senger of, 47, 61, 113,
  114, 116, 142, 144–146
  as last Messenger, 96, 111
  promised in Old Testament,
  141
  See also Muhammad, Elijah
 Fard as Prophet of, 47
  See also Fard, W. D.
 has no "son," 106–107
 Islam as religion of, 98
 a live God, 22, 108–110
 Paradise of, 142
 rebellion of Yakub against,
  55–57, 62
Allen, Richard, 38
And Then We Heard the Thunder, (novel), 41
Anti-Semitism
 Black Muslims and, 63, 172
 Christianity and, 64-65

Arabic language
 in Black Muslim services, 18
 taught in University of Islam,
  72
 used by Akbar Muhammad,
  85
Armageddon, Battle of, 19, 27,
 68
 Muhammad's teachings about,
  48
"As-Salaam-Alaikum," 18
Atlanta, Ga., 75
"Atlanta Speech" of Elijah Muhammad, 62, 95–111
Atlanta University, Malcolm
 X's speech at, 61, 134–
 146
Attucks, Crispus, 59

Baldwin, James, 67, 68, 170
Bannaker, Benjamin, 59
Baptist Church
 attacks slavery, 37
 Negro churches founded, 38,
  39
Bean pie, 17
Belafonte, Harry, 170
Bennett, Lerone, Jr., 32, 33
Bergson, Henri, 33
Bible
 Fard's use of, 42, 44
 quoted by Elijah Muhammad,
  103
 quoted by Malcolm X, 123,
  139–145, 165
 as theological basis of Ne-
  gro's "inferiority," 39,
  52, 105
 See also Christianity
"Big Red," see Malcolm X
Birmingham, Ala., 25, 178
 Black Muslim policy toward
  1963 demonstrations, 74–
  76, 78
 temple in, 18
Black, God as, 22, 55, 140
Black Bourgeoisie, 162–63
Black men
 must become fearless, 96,
  104, 105–106